M000044801

REIMAGINE RETIREMENT

REIMAGINE RETIREMENT

PLANNING AND
LIVING FOR THE
GLORY OF GOD

C. J.
CAGLE

B&H
PUBLISHING
NASHVILLE, TENNESSEE

Copyright © 2019 by Carl J. Cagle Jr.
All rights reserved.
Printed in the United States of America

978-1-5359-5417-4

Published by B&H Publishing Group
Nashville, Tennessee

Dewey Decimal Classification: 306.3
Subject Heading: RETIREES / RETIREMENT / ELDERLY

Unless otherwise noted, all Scripture quotations are taken from
the Christian Standard Bible®, Copyright © 2017 by Holman Bible
Publishers. Used by permission. Christian Standard Bible® and CSB®
are federally registered trademarks of Holman Bible Publishers.

Also used: English Standard Version (ESV). ESV® Text Edition: 2016.
Copyright © 2001 by Crossway Bibles, a publishing ministry of
Good News Publishers.

Also used: Holman Christian Standard Bible (HCSB), copyright
© 1999, 2000, 2002, 2003, 2009 by Holman Bible Publishers,
Nashville, Tennessee. All rights reserved.

Cover design by Matt Lehman.
Illustration by Alexander Baidin / Shutterstock.

1 2 3 4 5 6 7 • 23 22 21 20 19

CONTENTS

Part One: Reimagine Your
Perspective on Retirement

Part Two: Reimagine Your
Plan for Retirement

Part Three: Reimagine Your Life in Retirement

PREFACE

I have always been interested in personal finance. But I became especially interested in personal finance as a *christian* about 20 years ago, after attending a stewardship class at my church. Since then, I have been learning all I can about it and trying to apply it in my own life.

Eventually, I started ministering to others in various ways in the area of personal finances and stewardship, mainly in the context of my local church. A lot of the folks I have had the privilege to work with were middle-aged or older, so retirement planning is a frequent topic of discussion. I often find that they lack any sort of plan for retirement and would most likely not have the necessary resources to retire when the time comes.

On the other hand, I have seen a lot of older people with a plan for retirement go into it with a limited perspective on what living in retirement as a disciple of Jesus Christ should look like.

Because I wanted to help such people, and also because I was grappling with some of the same questions and concerns as I moved through my 50s and into my 60s, I started reading and studying extensively about retirement. Several years ago, I also started writing about it on a blog called *Retirement Stewardship* (www.retirementstewardship.com). Many of the books I read about retirement were focused mainly on either the personal aspects (physical, emotional, mental, and spiritual) or the financial areas (planning, saving, investing, and generating income in retirement), but not both. There was a need here.

My thinking has been influenced by writers such as John Piper (*Rethinking Retirement*) and Randy Alcorn (*The Treasure Principle*) who challenge us to reject the world's messages on retirement and instead look at it through the lens of biblical truth. I also found the many books and other materials from men like the late Larry Burkett, Dave Ramsey, Chris Hogan, Ron Blue, Chuck Bentley, and others who stress practicing wise biblical stewardship to be extremely helpful. The investing philosophies espoused by experts like Austin Pryor, John Templeton, John Bogle and The Bogle Heads, Ben Stein and Phil Demuth, and Paul Merriman were instrumental in forming my perspectives on investing and those that I present in this book. The expertise of others like Dr. Wade D. Pfau, a respected personal finance professor and retirement researcher, and Steve Vernon, FSA, a retired actuary and retirement planning professional, was beneficial as well. But I didn't find a lot of books about retirement that broadly addressed both the spiritual and practical concerns of older Christians as well as those of younger believers who want to wisely plan for the future.

This is why I wrote *Reimagine Retirement*. In this book, I discuss planning for and living in retirement based on biblical principles while also challenging some of the contemporary societal and cultural norms that can influence Christians in ways that are inconsistent with what Scripture teaches. Rather than envisioning retirement as 20 or 30 years of leisure and recreation—a concept that is nowhere to be found in Scripture—I wanted to present a compelling God-glorifying alternative that the reader can apply to their own situation.

That said, I want to make it clear that I don't think that the Bible is opposed to the enjoyment of leisure and recreation during retirement—they are good gifts from God. Instead of falling to the ditch on either side, I want us to think more deeply about how we should live in this stage of life in light of biblical teaching, and adjust our values and priorities accordingly.

I also need to state up-front that I am not, nor have I ever been, a financial professional, and do not consider myself to be a financial/retirement planning guru. I am just a fairly average, financially conservative guy who wants to steward my God-given resources well and who is making a lot of the same critical decisions about retirement that you are. My goal in writing this book is to help others deal with the challenges of planning for and living in retirement from a biblical perspective based on my own study and experience and what I have learned by working with others. I would also note that this book is in no way an exhaustive treatment of the subject. Whole books have been written on the topics of some chapters in this one (such as saving and investing). But I do my best to present a wide range of relevant and useful information in an easily digestible way.

My views on stewardship are pretty basic. I believe that the primary purpose of everything we have been given is to bring glory to God, which includes the personal enjoyment that we derive from using some of it for ourselves. I value simplicity over complexity, pragmatism over sophistication, and I believe that money is a gift from God and a means to an end, rather than an end in itself. In *Reimagine Retirement*, my goal is to lay before you a biblical and actionable vision for what a God-honoring and God-glorifying retirement would look like. I offer practical guidance founded on biblical stewardship principles that will help you reimagine *your* retirement.

> The primary purpose of everything we have been given is to bring glory to God.

Carl J. (Chris) Cagle Jr.
Charlotte, North Carolina
November 2019

ACKNOWLEDGMENTS

I have already acknowledged the many gifted Christian teachers and writers (Piper, Alcorn, Burkett, Ramsey, Blue, and others) who both inspired and informed my thinking on this subject. We are all indebted to them for the broad and deep foundations that they have laid that have benefited Christians all over the world.

To my wife, Joanne, who encouraged me every step of the way, thanks for your example as you faithfully and tirelessly serve our family and church community in so many ways. And also to my grown children, Matt and Melinda, thanks for your constant love and support. I love you all very much.

To my pastor friends who serve in my home church—Jeremy Oddy, JJ Psyche, and Joe Lechner—thank you for your encouragement and support. And particularly to my good friend and longtime senior pastor Mickey Connolly—who is now in his late 60s and continuing to faithfully serve our church and denomination—thank you for your words of encouragement from the very beginning and for the inspiration of your example of a life well-lived for the good of others and the glory of God.

To my fellow deacon and friend, Jeff Hutchinson, who read the original manuscript and provided many helpful suggestions and valuable input, and whose life embodies so many of the principles I discuss in this book.

To the many older Christians that I serve alongside at Crossway Community Church, like my friend and another fellow deacon, Gordon Howe, a retired airline pilot, who works on our church staff without pay as our full-time community outreach leader, thanks for all of the ways you inspire me.

To Ivan Mesa, books editor at The Gospel Coalition (TGC), who initially suggested that I consider writing a book on biblical steward-ship and provided practical assistance during the initial phase, I don't think this book would have become a reality without your help. And to Taylor Combs, my editor, and the great staff at B&H Publishing Group, thanks for believing that this book was worthy of the B&H name and for all the assistance along the way.

INTRODUCTION

Not long ago, I was having a conversation with a friend at church. He is about my age (mid-60s), and we were discussing retirement. Due to some medical challenges, he said that had been considering it, but he also said in so many words that the thought of it worries him. His apprehension is understandable.

As a stewardship coach in my local church, I have had similar conversations with others. Some are concerned that retirement will be unsettling and disorienting, or perhaps downright depressing, due to the lack of meaningful activity, engagement, and fulfillment that their work provides. Others would like to retire for one reason or another and have plans for how they want to spend their time, but are concerned that they haven't saved enough and, therefore, won't be provided for into their last years. And then there are those who just haven't thought about it very much, although I think they are in the minority.

Confusing and Conflicting Messages

Retirement can indeed be a complicated and overwhelming subject; the financial complexities alone are enough to make our heads swim. Society and popular culture, and the constant flood of information from the financial media influence the thoughts, emotions, and actions of many. But another reason the topic can be so unsettling is that we hear so many different, often conflicting, messages on the subject. For example, on the one hand, our culture has traditionally said this: Work hard at a job or career that you may or may not like, save and invest as much as you can, and then hopefully go on vacation for the last 20 or 30 years of your life if you can afford it. If not, hope the government and/or your family will take care of you. You worked for it, and you deserve it, so go for it; it's part of the "American Dream."

On the other hand, some Christians reject the idea of retirement altogether. They view it as a modern cultural phenomenon that isn't explicitly taught in the Bible and, therefore, should be avoided. While you may not work the same job forever, this group says, you must always be working for the Lord until the end in ways appropriate for your age and abilities.

And then there are those who don't see retirement as something that the Bible necessarily forbids but who reject many of the more popular viewpoints so prevalent in our day. They would say that even though our modern-day concept of retirement was unimaginable in biblical times (which is why the Bible doesn't say a lot about it in the first place), Scripture does have a lot to say about how Christians should live during all stages of life, including the time we call retirement. I would count myself among this third crowd.

Practical Challenges

Over the years, I have observed that many fellow Christians didn't have a vision or plan for retirement, or if they did, weren't sure how they would finance it (if it didn't involve working for pay). I have also been concerned as I watched as some older Christians withdrew from the mainstream of church and community life, becoming more and more self-focused in pursuing the pleasures of life rather than the furtherance of the kingdom of God due to an increasing sense of entitlement based on worldly ideals. I've also encountered many who had a financial plan but were surprised to learn that it might not be sufficient to fund an extended time in retirement.

This is a systemic problem. According to a recent study by a major accounting firm, almost 40 percent of employees over age 50 have $50,000 or less saved for retirement, and a third of them have nothing saved. Among the baby boomers, those who are nearing or already in retirement, the number falls to 32 percent! That means that a large percentage of middle-class Americans are on track to be living at or near the poverty line when they quit working, especially if they are forced to retire early due to reasons beyond their control. The study also said that the fear of possibly running out of money in retirement was the biggest concern for all those surveyed.[1]

Statistically, most people will retire in their early 60s, and almost everyone will retire eventually. To further complicate things, we are living longer and longer and may spend many years in retirement, more than previous generations. Unfortunately, many people do not prepare for such a long retirement and will not be able to enjoy the life they imagined, and others are in danger of not having the resources to meet their basic needs.

To help the reader address these challenges, I will tackle several major topics in this book pertaining to retirement planning that people tend to find complicated, confusing, and overwhelming, and present them in a straightforward and understandable way.

Three Main Goals

I have three main goals for this book:

First, that you will be inspired to reimagine a retirement that rejects modern worldly values and priorities and, realizing that God has called you for a higher purpose than the full-time pursuit of pleasure and self-fulfillment, instead reimagine a retirement focused on living for the glory and honor of God and the good of others.

Second, to help you wisely apply biblical principles and practices so you can reimagine a retirement with dignity—one with your essential spending needs met for as long as you live, perhaps with a surplus to share, while continually trusting in God as the ultimate source of your daily provision.

And third, if and when you decide to retire, to reimagine living it in a way that is consistent with kingdom principles—with paid or unpaid work, relationally focused activities, voluntary involvement and commitments in your church and community, and continued faithful devotion to God and his people, for as long as he gives you the ability to do so.

Disclaimer

The primary intent and purpose of this book are to provide guidance in the form of educational information related to Christian living and stewardship, personal financial and retirement planning, and living in retirement. Any information in regard to money, spending, credit, personal finance, investing, Social Security, taxes, or insurance, or in relation to any other monetary topic provided or shared in this book is, therefore, presented for information and entertainment purposes only and does not constitute professional financial advice for your specific situation or circumstances.

The information herein is given to you with the understanding that the author is NOT engaged in rendering any legal, accounting, business or personal financial or investment advice. As the information in this book is not professional advice, it should not be treated as such.

You and you alone are responsible for your financial decisions, and you are encouraged to seek professional advice before making any material changes to your finances or investments.

The educational information in this book is provided "as is" without any representations or warranties, express or implied. I make no representations or warranties concerning the educational information in this book.

Although I have made sincere and strong efforts to make sure the information is accurate, I cannot guarantee that all the information in this book is always correct, complete, or up-to-date.

The views and opinions expressed are mine. Any content provided by other authors or individuals referenced in this is their opinion, and is not intended to malign any religion, ethnic group, club, organization, company, individual, or anyone or anything.

Part One

REIMAGINE YOUR PERSPECTIVE ON RETIREMENT

Chapter 1

UNDERSTANDING MODERN RETIREMENT

"[Social Security] proposes, by means of old-age pensions, to help those who have reached the age of retirement to give up their jobs and thus give to the younger generation greater opportunities for work and to give to all, old and young alike, a feeling of security as they look toward old age." —*Franklin D. Roosevelt*

"Retirement at sixty-five is ridiculous. When I was sixty-five, I still had pimples." —*George Burns*

Nowadays, retirement is one of the most discussed topics around. The front page of almost every popular personal finance magazine and the home page of most financial websites regularly feature articles about it. Retirement is also a big business. An entire financial services industry exists to help us save and invest for retirement. Plus, we have retirement communities, retirement homes, and nursing centers springing up all over the place. We are a culture and a society obsessed with retirement—at the very least, it is top of mind for many people.

So how did it come to be such a part of our modern social fabric and culture? The answer is found in an interesting story of society, economics, government, corporations, mass media, unions, and people all conspiring to create the modern-day phenomenon we call *retirement*.

Before Retirement Was a Thing

The history of retirement as we know it is relatively short. It didn't exist in preindustrial America and only recently became possible in more prosperous nations whose people had increasingly long lifespans. In the late nineteenth century, over 75 percent of American men that reached age 64 or older were still in the workforce. Working was a sign of vitality and productiveness and retirement was considered undesirable and to be avoided unless it was forced due to ill health or disability. Even then, people may have pursued alternative types of work, not necessarily a total withdrawal from all productive activity.

Historically, in the United States and throughout the world older people relied on the support of family once they were unable to work. That is consistent with the Bible's teaching in 1 Timothy 5:3–4, 8 about caring for family members who aren't able to care for themselves.[1] In the early church and throughout history, Christians with family members who were in need were expected to help. But in our busy, modern age, caring for elderly parents can be a very challenging thing for a family to take on. Some do so in their homes, while others turn to assisted living centers or skilled nursing centers, helping with the costs if they are able.

Difficult though it may be, and regardless of the circumstances, children do have obligations to their parents who need financial assistance, or may be sick, or need a place to live. Even if they are under the care of someone else, such as a skilled nursing facility, families need to make sure their parents are lovingly and adequately cared for in facilities that are up to par. In doing so, children fulfill the biblical

requirement: "Honor your father and mother, which is the first commandment with a promise, so that it may go well with you and that
you may have a long life in the land" (Eph. 6:2–3).

Sadly, studies have shown that many older retirees in the US will
end up in pretty bad shape due to a lack of familial and financial
resources. According to the National Council on Aging, more than 25
million people over age 60 live at or below the federal poverty level,
which is $29,425 per person per year.[2]

Companies and Labor Unions Step In

Through the 1700s and most of the 1800s, most companies in
the United States were small or family-run businesses. But as industry
and commerce in the United States began to grow, larger companies
were formed, and businesses took a more active role by introducing
the first defined benefit pension plans. The first was established by
American Express in 1875. Workers who had been with the company
for 20 years and were at least age 60 could be considered to receive a
retirement pension of up to half of their annual salary or a maximum
of $500 per month.[3]

Key Concept: A *defined-benefit plan* is a type of employer-
sponsored retirement plan where benefits are provided
based on a calculation that uses multiple variables but
mainly the length of employment and salary history.
In most plans, the employer makes 100 percent of the
contributions and also manages the plan, which includes
portfolio management and investment risk. The company
administers portfolio management and investment risk
for the plan. Employees can only withdraw funds without
penalty under certain conditions.

The labor unions were also an emerging influence during this time as they had embraced the idea of retirement as a way of moving older workers out, thereby ensuring that younger members would have jobs (which was their promise to their newer members). In the early 1900s, the government started promoting pensions, and pension plan growth was further spurred by the Internal Revenue Act of 1921 because it gave a federal income tax exemption to company contributions made to employee pension funds. By 1950, about 10 million Americans—nearly 25 percent of the private sector workforce—had a pension. The number continued to grow and ten years later in 1960 about half of the private sector workforce had one, as did almost all public sector employees.

Social Security Appears on the Scene

On the heels of the Great Depression of the 1920s and '30s, over 50 percent of senior citizens were living in poverty. That led to the signing of the Social Security Act into law in 1935. The Social Security program was mainly designed to provide a type of old age insurance to the most vulnerable who were unable to work. At that time, the two most significant questions that needed answering were: Where would the money come from to pay for it, and when would someone be eligible to start receiving benefits?

Key Concept: *Social Security* is a welfare and insurance program set up and managed by the US government that pays annuity-like benefits to retirees, workers who become disabled, and survivors of deceased workers.

We know the answer to the first question: People who were still working would be taxed so that those who were retired could receive benefits. It was a controversial idea, and although the new tax was viewed with some skepticism, the majority of Americans viewed it favorably; Gallup polls showed more than two-thirds of those surveyed in 1936–37 approved of the program.[4]

The second question about when to provide benefits was more challenging to answer, but there was a precedent from Europe. In the late 1800s, German Chancellor Otto von Bismarck, citing Psalm 90:10, "Our lives last seventy years or, if we are strong, eighty years. Even the best of them are struggle and sorrow; indeed, they pass quickly and we fly away," set up a government disability program for those ages 70 and older, but very few lived that long. President Roosevelt and his New Dealers eventually settled on age 65 even though, in the United States, the average life expectancy at the time was 58 for men and 62 for women.[5] Therefore, many people didn't live long enough to receive their full benefits. Fast forward 70 years, and average lifespans are on the increase. They are now in the high 70s for men and low 80s for women.[6]

In 1951, the US Congress allowed employees of nonprofit organizations the option of being part of the Social Security program, but ministers were treated as self-employed under the law. Then, in 1955, ministers, who had been classified as self-employed, were given the option of entering the program but they had to pay the full tax for themselves. Eventually, in 1968, ministers were required by law to participate in Social Security. However, due to strong opposition from many denominations, Congress allowed ministers to opt out as a matter of religious conviction. Current law still technically requires ministers to pay the tax but provides for an opt-out provision as an exemption to the law. To opt-out on religious grounds, a minister must complete Social Security Form 4361.[7]

If we fast-forward from 1935—84 years later—the life expectancy of a reasonably healthy 65-year-old is now 78 and 83 for men and women respectively, but the full retirement age for most of us for Social Security is still 66 to 67.[8] Social Security has morphed from a program that provided benefits to a relatively small percentage of people into a fully institutionalized government program that will be heavily relied upon by the vast majority of older Americans to fund all or part of their retirement. In fact, data from the Social Security Administration (SSA) shows that 61 percent of retirees depend on their benefits to provide at least half of their monthly income. For older unmarried recipients, the number jumps to 71 percent.[9]

Retirement Savings Accounts Enter the Picture

By the early 1950s, people were able to combine their Social Security and pension incomes and fund a decent retirement lifestyle, even if they didn't live very long after they retired. It was at this time that the financial services industry began its mass-media campaigns that marketed retirement as a worker's good-and-just reward for his or her many years of loyalty and hard work. Retirement-oriented investment products started showing up on the scene, and they quickly became big business. Pensions and Social Security were the norm for many workers until the passage of the Revenue Act of 1978, which started the slow shift away from company-paid pension plans to defined contribution savings plans, commonly known as 401(k)/403(b)/457(b) plans, so named based on the applicable sections of the Internal Revenue Service (IRS) code.

Key Concept: *Defined-contribution plans* are retirement plans that are typically tax-deferred (taxes are not paid on earnings until they are withdrawn), like those that adhere to the 401(k), 403(b), and 457(b) sections of the IRS Code, which employees contribute a fixed amount or a percentage of their paychecks that is intended to fund their retirements. The sponsoring company (or government entity) will usually match a portion of employee contributions as an added employee benefit. Like defined-benefit plans, these plans also have restrictions on how and when employees can withdraw funds without penalties.

These would become the primary way that employees would save for their retirement, especially as many companies started scuttling their defined benefit (pension) plans in favor of the new defined-contribution plans that put more of the burden on the employees. Based on a recent Towers Watson study, only about 20 percent of Fortune 500 companies offered a defined benefit (pension) plan to new employees in 2015, down from just ten years ago in 2005 when more than 48 percent of the firms provided them.[10] The numbers continue to decrease as more companies seek to shift the burden more directly to employees, emphasizing the need for employees to take more responsibility for their retirement by leveraging these plans.

Retirement "Styles" Emerge

All of these things—pension plans, Social Security, tax-deferred and tax-free retirement savings accounts—have, somewhat intentionally it seems, resulted in a structured program of retirement in our society. Over the last 50 years, this somewhat artificial and socially programmed plan for retirement has resulted in the emergence of a variety of different modern retirement styles, each with its own timing and objectives.

Traditional Retirement

According to a 2018 Gallup poll, "The average reported retirement age for Americans who are currently retired is 61, considerably lower than the age at which current non-retirees say they will retire" (which is age 66 or older).[11] The traditional retirement age is 65 years old and has its origins in the original Social Security Act; 65 was considered full retirement age. As a result, someone who reaches age 65 is considered "old."

I bet you know some 65-year-olds who are more active and engaged than some 45-year-olds! Even if some of their body parts don't function as well as they used to, they are still active and involved with family, friends, church, and community; it's also very possible they are still working in some capacity. So, as it turns out, a fixed-age retirement is an artificial construct. With the recent gains in health and longevity during the twentieth century, 62 or 65 seem to be very arbitrary ages for a person to stop working when so many remain strong and able well into their 70s.[12]

This retirement style has been fostered by improved health, longer life, and a generally more affluent population. Thus, there has been a definite shift from disability- or obsolescence-caused retirement to one focused on the pursuit of leisure and recreation. The idealized view, which is often conveyed through magazine and TV ads, is that you can have a luxurious, pleasure-filled retirement if you get a good job, work hard enough and long enough (perhaps 30 or 40 years, or longer), and save enough. In other words, if you want it to be, your retirement can be a long, permanent vacation. According

> **A fixed-age retirement is an artificial construct.**

to this vision, if you have all three legs of the retirement stool (Social Security, employer pension, personal savings) working for you, you have a good chance of making this a reality. If not, you may have some challenges.

Early Retirement

The main idea here is that achieving financial independence (FI) is a worthy life goal that you can reach sooner rather than later if you are willing to work hard, live frugally, and save aggressively. The earlier you can retire, the freer you will be to do whatever you want for the rest of your life.

One of the significant differences between early retirement and a more traditional one is the required saving rate. Retirement at age 65 or 66 requires a saving rate of 10 to 15 percent over a lifetime (or maybe 20% if you start late). The early retirement model requires you to be much more aggressive, perhaps saving half your income or more. Young workers will have to make significant sacrifices to retire much sooner than their 50s or 60s. Plus, leaving the working world too early can be unwise. You need to count the cost as it will take a lot of money to support you and your family for 50 or 60 years in retirement.[13]

On the other hand, if it is financially feasible for you to retire early, it can be a worthy goal if you intend to free up your time for service to God and others. But if you have to work so much that you can't be generous with your time, or you have to save so much that you can't be generous with your money, then you may want to reconsider.

There is something noble and commendable about making sacrifices to be able to retire early so that you can do something that you are genuinely passionate about, but biblically, there are some flaws here. As Christians, our passion is to live our lives for the Savior, and we can do that in whatever setting God has placed us. The early retirement crowd is mainly focused on personal passions that are about self-fulfillment and satisfaction, which may include the good of others, but not necessarily the glory of God.

Semi-Retirement

This is based on the changing dynamics of the traditional retirement model and the idea that, while retirement can be fun and rewarding, balancing work of some kind—either for pay or not—and leisure may result in a more positive and fulfilling life. The traditional idea of retirement is becoming less and less attractive and affordable as well. In fact, about 25 percent of baby boomers say they aren't satisfied with retirement.[14] In a way, that is good news, as it was never a great idea to begin with. As a result, a growing number of retirees are seeking ways to stay active and busy doing some kind of "work" even after retirement from their full-time jobs. Retirees realize that not engaging in any kind of productive activity is dangerous to their overall health and well-being.

Recent studies paint a slightly brighter picture of contemporary retirement as people shy away from a traditional retirement. For example, a recent survey by Age Wave/Merrill Lynch found that 73 percent of retirees plan to work, either full- or part-time or intermittently, in retirement.[15] The study also found that the fastest-growing segment in the US workforce is age 55 and older. This idea of retirement as "flex-time"—part-time work or occasional full-time work—is gaining traction. Semi-retirees who want to stay in their field but work less are finding that consulting or project-related work are good options for the latter.

No Retirement

This is not the most common option since most of us will retire sometime and the majority of people gravitate toward one style or the other, no matter what our work situation is. Each has its positives and negatives, and each can be considered and evaluated in light of biblical principles. What retirement looks like for you will depend on how you apply those principles in your unique situation.

What about the Retirement "Crisis"?

In spite of all the private and government programs created to help people prepare for retirement, there is a widespread belief that most Americans will be woefully unprepared for it when the time comes. The word *crisis* is bantered around rather freely as though retirees by the millions are running headlong toward some financial cliff of certain fiscal ruin. Those who hold this view would say that too many are at risk of not having enough money to maintain a reasonable standard of living in retirement, or that their money won't last long enough, and that the problem is only getting worse.

One way that retirement professionals like to frame the problem is by describing the "three-legged stool" of retirement consisting of Social Security, traditional defined benefit (pension) plans, and personal savings (defined contribution plans) as shown in Figure 1. Someone who has all three going for them in retirement is in pretty good shape. But those who believe we are headed toward a crisis warn that the stool is becoming increasingly shaky. The oldest "leg," the traditional pension, is fast becoming a relic of a previous age. Good luck trying to find an employer that still offers them; they just can't afford them any longer. If you're looking for a nice fat pension with great health-care benefits on the side, you'd better go to work for a local, state, or federal government entity.

FIGURE 1: The "Three-Legged Stool" of Traditional Retirement

Next, there's the concern about the long-term viability of Social Security, which is a never-ending topic of discussion and speculation by political and financial types. Full retirement age is gradually climbing, but it remains far below average lifespans, which, thanks to the common graces of modern medicine, continue to increase. Some want benefits reduced, and others think they need to be increased. Regardless, it is increasingly likely that Social Security will undergo significant change in the not-so-distant future, and may become a less certain source of retirement income.

The three-legged stool for retirement now has two wobbly legs, which brings us to personal savings, the third leg of the retirement stool. As companies have moved away from traditional pension plans (in which they paid most or all of the premiums), they have happily switched to defined contribution plans such as 401(k)s and other similar plans that put much more of the saving burden on you and me. Given the cutbacks and uncertainty elsewhere, this needs to be the strongest leg of our retirement stool. But as we shall see, it is also a little wobbly.

There is one more "leg" that isn't usually discussed as part of the three-legged stool that many people are counting on to help them in retirement: a large inheritance. There are good reasons for this. Some predictions say that trillions (with a "T") of dollars will transfer from the oldest generation over the next few decades. One study found that older families in the United States plan to leave an average estate of $177,000.[16] That would indeed be a huge windfall for many.

The problem is that anticipated inheritances don't always play out as you expect. Older people change their minds. Or, they have to spend a lot of their money on health care or long-term nursing care. Some will live a long, long time, perhaps well into their 90s, and will use up all their savings. Others are cheated out of their money, sometimes sadly by a family member or friend, or a dishonest financial professional. Therefore, it would be wise not to presume on a big inheritance and plan accordingly; if one does materialize, then all the better.

We saw in the previous section that while worker *participation* in retirement savings plans is relatively high, overall saving *amounts* may not be sufficient. Recent studies and statistics seem to bear this out, such as the PwC study I cited in the introduction, and further support is provided by a 2017 Retirement Confidence Survey by the Employee Benefit Research Institute. It found that about half of workers said they had less than $25,000 in savings, and about half of this group had less than $1,000 saved.[17] Other studies have shown that many households headed by someone age 55 or older had neither a tax-deferred savings account nor were they covered by a pension plan. That meant that Social Security could be their only source of income in retirement unless they continued to work.[18]

In spite of these concerning numbers, others are not convinced. While it's true that many may not be able to maintain their preretirement standard of living, some contend that most retirees do not need to sustain a standard of living that is 100 percent of what they enjoyed before retirement. According to the Bureau of Labor Statistics, an average couple in their mid-60s with no children at home will spend about $48,000 a year, which is less than the US Census median household income of $57,000. If a retired couple needs 80 percent of median income to live, and Social Security replaces approximately 40 percent of median income, that leaves about $27,000, or 40 percent, that needs to be covered by a pension, annuity, or savings.

So is there a coming retirement crisis or not? Well, it may be inaccurate to say that *all* Americans are facing a retirement crisis, but it does appear that a significant percentage of the retired population will have challenges. One study that presents a more middle-of-the-road finding is the National Retirement Risk Index (NRRI), which is done by the Center for Retirement Research. Based on the NRRI, 50 percent of retirees *could* have problems that may require them to save more or work longer, or lower their standard of living if possible, which may be feasible for some.[19] If 25 percent of them can do so, then 25 percent will remain at-risk. Other studies convincingly estimate that the share of households without sufficient assets in retirement stands at slightly more than 50 percent. But even more sobering is the fact that the most optimistic studies still find that nearly one-quarter of retirees are falling short. There can be little doubt that there is a lack of saving such that approximately 25 percent, and perhaps as many as 50 percent, will have some financial risk in retirement. The amount of risk may vary based on when you retire and what kind of lifestyle you have imagined in retirement.

Having taken a look at how retirement came to play such an important role in contemporary life, in the next chapter, we will turn our attention to what the Bible says (and doesn't say) about it. We need a biblical perspective on such an important topic, and as we shall see, retirement isn't a major subject in Scripture. Fortunately, that doesn't mean that God isn't concerned about it, nor does it mean he has nothing to say to us about it. As is so often the case, the Bible is full of helpful wisdom and guidance that we can apply to all stages of life, including retirement.

Summary

- Retirement is a modern social institution that was virtually unknown before the twentieth century and most commonly found in prosperous Western countries.

- Many different social, political, and economic forces converged to conceive, construct, and perpetuate the phenomenon we know as *retirement*.

- In many ways, retirement is an artificial construct because it was not necessitated by an inability to work but rather an arbitrary age.

- There are several different modes of retirement, the most common of which is a traditional retirement between the age of 60 and 70.

- The traditional understanding of retirement is a prolonged period of leisure and recreation followed by cognitive and physical decline.

- Many retirees will continue to work productively and contribute to the world around them, just not necessarily for pay, or for as much pay.

- Although the retirement crisis can be overblown at times, there can be no doubt that a large number will face significant financial challenges in retirement.

For Reflection

- In what ways did your grandfather's or great-grandfather's retirement look different from what is common today?

- What is your perception of retirement? Do you hold to a traditional view or something else?

- At what age do you plan to retire? Why did you choose that age in particular?

Chapter 2

WHAT THE BIBLE SAYS ABOUT RETIREMENT

"Work is so foundational to our makeup that it is one of the few things we can take in significant doses without harm. Indeed, the Bible does not say we should work one day and rest six or that work and rest should be balanced evenly but directs us to the opposite ratio. Leisure and pleasure are great goods, but we can take only so much of them." —Tim Keller

"The one principle that surrounds everything else is that of stewardship; that we are the managers of everything that God has given us." —Larry Burkett

As Christians, we need to evaluate contemporary topics and issues in light of the teachings of Scripture so that we can answer the question: "How should we then live?" Fortunately, the Bible has a lot to say about many things that are relevant to our everyday lives. God knows exactly what we need and, in his Word, he ". . . has given us everything required for life and godliness through the knowledge of him who called us by his own glory and goodness" (2 Pet. 1:3). But, perhaps not surprisingly given the modernity of the topic, the Bible says very little about retirement, which has become such a big part of our modern social, economic, and political landscape. We must not conclude, however, that the Bible doesn't provide us with any insight or guidance on the topic at all.

Retirement Wasn't Part of the Biblical Landscape

The reason for the Bible's silence on this topic should be pretty apparent: culture and society in biblical times were very different than they are now, as were life expectancy and family and work life. In Bible times, family and work were closely related; multigenerational households often engaged in the same types of work and children took care of their aging parents. In Old Testament times, most people worked as long as they could on the farm and then transitioned to less strenuous work if they had physical difficulties, either due to illness or injury or natural aging. This transition was much easier if they had children or servants who could pick up the slack for them. Retirement as we know it wasn't in the picture.

In New Testament Hellenistic and Roman societies, the economy was more varied and complex. Global trade was on the scene, and there were more types of occupations due to growing urban population centers. Although there was a large aristocracy, most families were poor, lived in adverse conditions, and had significant hygiene and nutrition problems. Many still farmed and, for most, life was hard. Life expectancy at birth during this time was 20 to 30 years. If someone reached age 10 (no easy task, apparently), it increased to 45 to 47 years. Although someone may have reached age 50 or 60 or more during those times, it was rare.[1]

Many things in our modern life aren't explicitly mentioned or addressed in the Bible. Words like *movie*, *social media*, or *cell phone* can't be found, since, like the modern concept of *retirement*, they didn't exist when the Bible was written. Even though the Bible says much about related topics such as money and possessions (which are mentioned over 800 times), and work and rest (which is mentioned almost as much), the subject of retirement is conspicuously absent.

So where does this leave us? If the Bible doesn't say anything explicitly about retirement, does it say anything at all about it?

> **Key Concept:** *Biblical principles* are truths that God has provided through his Word to help teach us how to live based on right thinking and behavior.

I believe we can learn a great deal from the Bible about retirement. Absent specific rules or instructions in Scripture, we have to look for the underlying principles, ideals, and values that are most relevant to our topic. Fundamental life principles, such as stewardship, can be distilled by examining multiple Bible verses in context. However, we must be careful only to associate a principle with a verse if it is part of the verse's originally intended meaning; in other words, what was intended by the author at the time it was written. Such principles are relevant throughout time and can be applied even in a modern context.[2]

In this chapter, we will consider the single reference to retirement in Scripture and also examine the cycle of work and rest, and the all-important stewardship principle, as these seem to be the ones most relevant to understanding retirement in light of biblical teaching.

Retirement in the Bible

The only specific mention of retirement in the Bible is in the Old Testament under the Law of Moses. The Levites (priests) had to retire from their work in the tabernacle at age 50. "But at fifty years old he is to retire from his service in the work and no longer serve" (Num. 8:25). I wonder how they came up with age 50. Abraham, Isaac, and Jacob all lived to be over 100. Isaac lived the longest of the three, to age 180. Age 50 seems young to retire from temple duty, but there was a good reason why the priests retired at age 50—they made room for the priestly interns who needed to learn the ropes.

After they retired, the older priests would not quit working altogether; they would stay on as instructors and mentors. So, this wasn't really retirement at all, as we understand it; it was a new job description. Being a priest back then was pretty hard work, even though it was a part-time job. Not only did they care for the tabernacle and its furnishings, but they also taught and served as judges. And even if they did not stay at the temple, they likely returned to Levitical towns and served in various capacities there until they died.

Other than the Levitical priests, we can find no other references to the older retiring to make way for the young in the Bible. What we do see are people serving the Lord very late in life.

In the New Testament, as you might suspect, Jesus and the apostles had nothing directly to say about retirement. The disciples didn't have a retirement plan; they expended their lives in service to the Master. Most died fairly young, often as martyrs, with the exception of John who was probably in his 60s or 70s when he wrote Revelation. We see a wide range of ages in the New Testament church, and in Titus 2 we read Paul's instruction to older men and women on how to disciple younger believers, implying that there were a significant number of older believers in the church (vv. 2–3).

The Principles of Work and Rest

The Bible has much more to say about work and rest than about retirement, and this content is relevant to our discussion, since retirement is by definition a cessation of work (or at least certain kinds of work and its level of intensity or duration).[3] These principles can be easily applied to the concept of retirement.

Work and Rest Were Originated by God

The ideas and activities of work and rest did not originate with us; they came from God himself. In Genesis chapters one and two we see how God creates and then sustains the physical world. As Tim Keller points out, "work was not a necessary evil . . . or something that humans were created to do that was beneath God . . . no, God worked for the sheer joy of it."[4]

After God had perfectly created the world and Adam and Eve to inhabit it, he shared the ongoing work of caring for his creation with them when he put Adam in charge of the garden to "work it and watch over it" (Gen. 2:15). Because sin had yet not entered the picture, the job that God gave to Adam was not to start toiling in the hot sun; it was more expansive and fruitful than that. God made Adam a steward, an overseer of all that he had made. Adam was the president of the Garden of Eden Country Club.

We also know from Genesis 2:2–3 that after creation God rested. But he didn't lie down and take a nap, since God doesn't get tired as we do. His was a different kind of rest, a cessation of work for no other reason than he was finished with the job of creating the universe and everything in it and took a step back to enjoy all that he had done. This was a "Godly relishing" of what he had accomplished; God the Father enjoyed the beauty and wonder of all he had made.

Work and Rest Are Good

In the Old Testament, God gave particular instructions to mankind about work. This is very evident in Exodus 20:8–10 where God commanded us to work for six days and reserve the seventh for rest, just as he did in creation. There is also a clear expectation in the New Testament that we will work, just as Jesus and his disciples did (2 Thess. 3:10–12). Paul condemned idleness and encouraged honest labor so that he and the other disciples would not be a burden to anyone (2 Thess 3:6–8). Hard work is given as the way of providing for oneself and one's family (Prov. 12:11; 14:23; 1 Tim. 5:4, 8). In fact, the Bible warns that refusing to work can lead to poverty, a lack of the most basic necessities (Prov. 10:4–5).

God wants us to work hard with the strength and abilities he provides. He gave work to us as one of the most necessary yet satisfying and fulfilling things we can do.

Work is good for us and also for the needy as evidenced in a command in Leviticus 23:22, where God tells Israel to work hard for a harvest, but to leave a portion for "the poor and the resident alien." This theme is reiterated in the New Testament when the apostle Paul identifies work as one of the ways we can show love to our neighbors when he said we should work "so that he has something to share with anyone in need" (Eph. 4:28b). He also said that it can be a way to gain the respect of non-Christian coworkers and to help support Christian ministries (1 Thess. 4:12; 1 Cor. 9:7–12; Gal. 6:6). It is in those ways and others that Paul says our work honors and glorifies God.

But work must be balanced with rest. In his wisdom, God knew that we would need rest. So, in the Old Testament, he gave the fourth commandment, which said that the Israelites were to work for six days out of the week, but were not to work on the seventh, the Sabbath day. In fact, Exodus 20:11b says that, "the LORD blessed the Sabbath day and declared it holy." God also instituted the yearlong Sabbath, which occurred every seventh year, and was to let not only the people but even the land rest. This solidified the wisdom of the natural cycles of work and rest that an infinite God knows we need as his finite creatures.

Work, Rest, and Retirement

Following the biblical wisdom of work and rest leads us to work "enthusiastically, as something done for the Lord and not for men" (Col. 3:23 HCSB), but also take time away from work to rest and recharge our physical, emotional, mental, and spiritual batteries. As shown in Figure 2, Christians do this by observing a Sunday Lord's Day, sometimes taking brief periods away from work (vacations), and occasionally taking extended times away (sabbaticals).

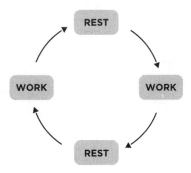

FIGURE 2: The Biblical Cycle of Work and Rest

These rhythms of work and rest become more necessary as we age. God gives us physical rest because he knows the nature of our humanity; we have inherent weaknesses and limitations, which increase with natural aging (Ps. 127:2). "He knows what we are made of, remembering that we are dust" (Ps. 103:14). Therefore, most of us will not be able to do certain kinds of work for our entire lives; our bodies just won't let us. Isaiah 40:6–8 reminds us of the reality that our earthly bodies are like grass and with the beauty and wonder of flowers in the field, which will eventually wither and fade.

> God gives us physical rest because he knows the nature of our humanity; we have inherent weaknesses and limitations, which increase with natural aging (Ps. 127:2).

But in spite of the constraints on the kinds of work we can do as we age, there is no discernable biblical pattern for three or four decades of work followed by two or three more decades of rest (retirement) unless it is brought on by disability or illness. It is clear that work is part of God's good design, typically followed by cessation of work for a time, followed by a return to work. The Sabbaths and festivals in the Bible came to an end when the people returned to work; they were not an endless vacation. As we age, the duration and intensity of the work we do may change, and we may need to work less and rest more, but that doesn't mean we stop working altogether.

All of the Bible's talk about work and rest should lead us to an increased spiritual rest, which actually has very little to do with whether we are working or not. Spiritual rest is resting in God, especially all that he has done for us in Christ. It is the rest that Jesus spoke of when he said: "Come to me, all of you who are weary and burdened, and I will give you rest" (Matt. 11:28). From a theological perspective, the Sabbath rest of the Old Testament points mainly to the gospel of the New Testament, through which we are saved, not by our works but by through faith, trusting in the grace of God in which we can find rest for our souls (Heb. 4:9–11).

The Stewardship Principle

Another biblical principle that is applicable to the subject of retirement is *stewardship*. When some people see that word, they immediately think of tithing, the latest building fund campaign, or perhaps the preacher's annual "money talk." But it's much broader than that; it's "the administration of duties or goods in one's care."[5]

Historically, in biblical times, a steward was hired by the owner of a house to care for it and manage its affairs. He was responsible for all the associated properties and resources and ensuring that they were maintained and used appropriately in the service of the master. In our context, God is the Master, and we are his stewards, overseeing all that he places in our care.

Stewardship is based on the foundational biblical truth of God's absolute ownership of all he has made. Although we are inclined to think of our money, our possessions, or our abilities, we don't own anything; God owns it all! Each of us, and everything we see and everything we have, were created by God, not us, so it all belongs to him. "The earth and everything in it, the world and its inhabitants, belong to the LORD" (Ps. 24:1).

We first see this principle in the creation story of Genesis 1 thru 3 where God gave Adam and Eve the mandate to take dominion over the physical/material realm. He didn't give them ownership of the world, only the responsibility of managing it on his behalf.

Sadly, their faithful stewardship didn't last long. Once sin entered the picture, the perfect relationship between Adam and Eve, God, and his creation all changed—sin had broken in and cursed everything. Not only so, but in a sense, sin entered the world because of Adam and Eve's failure as stewards. They were placed in charge of all that God had created—including animals and plants. But how did they fall into sin? By listening to an animal who told them they should eat from a plant. Poor stewardship wrecked the world.

But in spite of the enormous problems created by the Fall, we are no less God's stewards now than Adam and Eve were then; sin has just made our job much more difficult (Gen. 3:17).

We also see the stewardship principle in the New Testament where it is applied more specifically to our money and possessions, and also to our possession of the gospel of grace and all the spiritual gifts we have received from God (1 Cor. 4:1–2; Eph. 3:1–6; 1 Pet. 4:10). Stewardship under the New Covenant is based on the lordship of Christ and his rightful claim to every area of our lives, and also the grace that is at work in us and instructs us "to live in a sensible, righteous, and godly way in the present age" (Titus 2:12).

Stewardship certainly concerns how we manage our money and possessions—our treasure, if you will—but as shown in Figure 3, it includes much more. It refers to how we handle *all* the gifts God has given us, not just the material ones. All our wealth belongs to God, but so do the talents and special abilities we have been given. Our gifts could be spiritual, physical, intellectual, and even emotional. God gives us these gifts not just for our enjoyment and good, but also for the benefit of others and ultimately for his glory. As Jesus himself said, "Freely you received, freely give" (Matt. 10:8b).

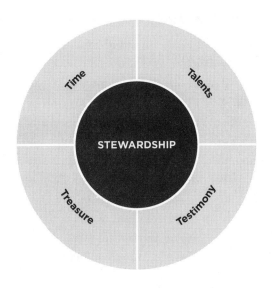

FIGURE 3: Stewardship

No matter what season of life we are in, we are called to be stewards of our:

- **Time**—"making the most of the time, because the days are evil" (Eph. 5:16).
- **Talents**—"Based on the gift each one has received, use it to serve others, as good managers of the varied grace of God" (1 Pet. 4:10 HCSB).
- **Testimony**—"as servants of Christ and managers of God's mysteries" (1 Cor. 4:1).
- **Treasure**—"From everyone who has been given much, much will be required; and from the one who has been entrusted with much, even more will be expected" (Luke 12:48).

Stewardship of Our Time

God is eternal and exists outside of time, but our time on this earth is limited, like a vapor that appears and then is gone (James 4:14). Therefore, we need to see ourselves as stewards of whatever time God gives us on earth. We really can't think about my time or your time; it's all God's, it all belongs to him, and we have a responsibility to redeem the time God has given us by making good use of it, and by "[paying] careful attention, then, to how [we] live—not as unwise people but as wise" (Eph. 5:15). For many, retirement can provide more time to serve others and work for the sake of the kingdom. On the other hand, it can provide a whole lot of time to waste. We must steward it carefully.

The best way to prepare for faithful stewardship of your time in retirement is careful thought, planning, and prayer, plus practical things like living within our means, saving and investing wisely, and regularly giving of our time *before* we retire; in other words, a lifestyle of stewardship. Cultivate habits of good stewardship before you are retired, so that you'll continue those habits then. That being said, any planning we do must be based on absolute dependence on God's kind providence and the recognition that he is sovereign over everything, including retirement. We plan and prepare in faith, not presumption (Prov. 27:1; James 4:13–16).

Stewardship of Our Talents

God tells us that we have been "fearfully and wonderfully made" (Ps. 139:14 esv). In fact, despite all the advances of modern science, we barely understand the marvelous complexity and diversity that we humans possess. He has made each of us unique and endowed us with just the right set of abilities and talents, with the intent that we would use them in service to others and for his glory (1 Pet. 4:10).

Some people may think they have no talents or gifts, but that simply isn't true. God has graciously given us various gifts, some more than others, according to his divine plan (1 Cor. 12:4–11), but all for the same purpose—for our enjoyment and his glory. He will never judge us on the amount of talent we have, only whether we used it for his purposes or not. The highest calling and purpose we have in this life is to use the gifts and abilities we have been given in service to the King for as long as we are able.

Stewardship of Our Testimony

Testimony is a fairly uncommon term; it usually only comes up in specific situations. It has a legal connotation in a courtroom setting. But in a Christian context, what does it really mean? The *Merriam Webster Dictionary* says that the two simplest definitions are "proof or evidence that something exists or is true" and "a formal written or spoken statement, especially one given in a court of law." So, in apologetics, a testimony (or witness) can be used to try to argue that God exists when others are arguing against his existence.

This kind of testimony is a common form, and it was very prevalent during early church history due to the number of eyewitnesses that were still around. The *Evangelical Dictionary of Theology*'s definition of *testimony* is a little different. It describes it as what is "to be given [by the Christian] centered on the facts of the meaning of the earthly ministry of Jesus (Acts 10:39–42) and his saving power (Acts 10:43)."[6] It goes on to describe how one faithful witness passes the knowledge to another, who gives it to another, and so forth. Our testimony today differs from those who were eyewitnesses to these things when Jesus was on the earth. It is based on the knowledge that has been passed on to us in Scripture and our individual experience of the grace of salvation through faith in Jesus Christ and transformative power of the Holy Spirit in our lives. Therefore, to steward our testimony is to hold fast to our personal witness to the truth of the gospel and its saving power throughout our lives. Our radically changed lives, perhaps most important, provide additional evidence that our testimony is authentic and genuine.

Even though our testimony involves us and comes from us, it's not about us, no matter how dramatic it may be. In the same way that we have been given gifts and possessions and talents, we have been given a testimony to share with others to point them to Christ and to glorify God. When we are older and perhaps living in retirement, stewardship of our testimony means that we are witness to his faithfulness throughout our lives. Beginning with our salvation, but also through times of pain and suffering as he continues to strengthen us with his glorious power and might to give us endurance, with joy, so that we may share one day in the inheritance of the saints (Col. 1:11–12). Character and perseverance are an essential part of a God-glorifying retirement.

Stewardship of Our Treasure

Successfully planning for and living in retirement is dependent on an appropriate level of financial preparedness, which can be accomplished through wise stewardship. The Bible instructs us to prepare for an uncertain future, like Joseph storing up food in preparation for a future famine in Genesis 41 and the description of the industrious ant storing up provisions for the future in Proverbs 6. It is wise to set something aside and invest it for a time when we are no longer able to work, or because we want to do something different but not necessarily for pay. But it is also vital to keep in mind that whatever material wealth we may accumulate toward that end will not transfer into eternity; only what is stored up as "treasure in heaven" (Luke 12:33) will survive. If we have stored up treasure on earth but have made few deposits in heaven, we will die as rich fools (Luke 12:13–21).

Therefore, rather than holding on tight to what we have, we are to give to the work of the kingdom and share with others in need. There are many, many verses in the Bible about having a heart of generosity and being willing to give. In 2 Corinthians 9:7, the apostle Paul tells us that we are to give, ". . . not reluctantly or out of necessity, for God loves a cheerful giver" (HCSB). I learned many years ago that stewarding your treasure doesn't have so much to do with how much you give, but with the attitude of your heart and relationship with God. This is just as true in retirement as it is when you are in your peak working and earning years.

Retirement: A Time to Steward All of God's Good Gifts Well

I would summarize stewardship of retirement as follows: using all the good gifts that God has generously given you for your joy, the good of others, and God's honor and glory, as you plan for and then live in retirement.[7] This view of the stewardship of later life requires rethinking and reorienting our choices, decisions, and resources in alignment with God's purposes and priorities—in other words, reimagining retirement. As good stewards, we will faithfully use all that God has given us—opportunities, interests, skills, jobs, family, friends, talents, spiritual gifts, possessions, health, and money—for godly purposes throughout our lives.

In the next chapter, we will look at some of the specific ways that the stewardship of our time, talents, treasure, and testimony in retirement can bring us joy and fulfillment, contribute to the good of others, and further God's kingdom on earth, thereby bringing honor and glory to God as we live for him.

Summary

- The Bible addresses many topics that are relevant to our everyday lives, but some modern subjects, such as retirement, aren't explicitly discussed.

- We have to rely on certain timeless biblical principles that can be applied to specific topics in our modern age.

- The Bible doesn't prohibit retirement, but there is also no precedent for several decades at the end of life focused only on leisure and recreation.

- The Bible teaches that we should live our lives consistent with the biblical principles of work and rest and stewardship, no matter what season of life we are in.

- Stewardship of retirement includes our time, talents, treasure, and testimony.

For Reflection

- What does it look like for you to practice work/ rest balance? How are you doing in that area, and what changes might you need to make?

- Do you view your time, talents, treasure, and testimony through the lens of biblical steward-ship? What can you do to align your life with that principle better?

- If you are close to retirement, does your view of it align more with the world or one based on the stewardship principle?

Chapter 3

IMAGINING A GOD-GLORIFYING RETIREMENT

"God has a plan for your retirement." —Billy Graham

"There is the built-in dignity of labor in the Scripture, and God calls me to labor in his vineyard until I die. It may not be at one particular job, but I have to be actively productive as long as I possibly can." —R. C. Sproul

At this point, you may be a little confused. In the first two chapters, I have tried to convince you that many of the modern views, values, and goals of retirement may not be God's plan for your life. I discussed how the Bible teaches that we were created to work in some form for as long as we are able, to rest at times, and that biblical stewardship of our time, talents, testimony, and treasure is an overarching biblical principle that will maximize our service to God and others. So, why am I even discussing retirement, and why devote several subsequent chapters to planning for, and living in, it? Don't we just need to retire retirement? Rather than dismissing it altogether, my goal is to challenge you instead to reimagine how you think about, plan for, and live in retirement based on biblical principles.

> **Key Concept:** A *reimagined retirement* is one that is planned, structured, lived, and continually reexamined in light of sound biblical doctrine, principles, and practice. It is a retirement lived for the glory of God, his kingdom, and the good of his people.

Our modern-day cultural, economic, and social context is very different than what it was in the times the Bible was written. The Bible doesn't tell us how its truths apply in specific cultures; instead, it gives us the freedom to apply those truths in different ways in a variety of cultures without altering the truths themselves to fit the culture.

While I have concluded that work (especially kingdom work) should remain an important part of an older Christian's life and that leisure and recreation are gifts from God but not meant to be our primary aim in life, we are nonetheless free to implement these biblical truths to our cultural concept of retirement.[1] This is what theologians call *contextualization*, applying the Bible's truths to a specific *context*. Larry Burkett and Ron Blue offer a good way to approach this: "We recommend viewing retirement as an adventure-filled next phase of life. Expect to work and seek meaningful work. Even if God has blessed you with adequate resources so that you need never work again, why waste your talents?"[2]

The biblical teaching on work and rest and the stewardship principle can apply to people in different ways at different times of their lives, so retirement will look different for different people. But no matter what our circumstances in life, it is the transforming power of the gospel—the Good News about Jesus Christ—that will have the most significant effect on our thoughts, attitudes, and actions. If the Christian's retirement is characterized by gospel centrality—meaning that saving faith in Christ has resulted in an inward transformation through the indwelling and empowering of his Holy Spirit—then all areas of life will be impacted, including the stage of life we call *retirement*.

The Gospel and Retirement

If we accept the idea retirement is permissible, and indeed not explicitly prohibited in Scripture, then we are presented with some challenging questions. Not the least of these is: How should we then live in retirement?

As with all areas of the Christian life, we must begin with the gospel as revealed in the Word of God. Once we believe, we receive all of the grace "given to each one of us according to the measure of Christ's gift" (Eph. 4:7). This gospel of grace is central because it "is the power of God for salvation to everyone who believes" (Rom. 1:16a) and because believing the gospel transforms us from the inside out and gives us a new life in Christ, which affects everything about us: "Therefore, if anyone is in Christ, he is a new creation; the old has passed away, and see, the new has come" (2 Cor. 5:17).

> **Key Concept:** The *gospel* is the good news of what God has done for us through Christ. It is the message of the salvation that we can receive by believing and trusting in the birth, life, death, and resurrection of Jesus Christ, the Son of God. The gospel is the power to save us from our sins, to place us in union with Christ and to give us a relationship with him, and also to cause us to walk in a new way of life (as new creations in Christ) as it transforms us from within.

We receive salvation by first hearing, understanding, and believing the gospel, and then responding to God's earnest plea, and finally by heartfelt repentance and faith in Christ alone for salvation. This salvation gives us the promise of eternal life, but it is more than that. The gospel not only changes our eternal destination, it also transforms our hearts and minds in the here and now. It changes our relationship to God, which is the best news of all, but it also transforms our relationship to everything else, including how we use our time, talents, testimony, and treasure for the sake of the gospel. Thus begins our new life in Christ as "we are transformed in every part of our minds, hearts, and lives by believing the gospel more and more deeply as life goes on."[3] As we believe, love, worship, follow, and obey Jesus, he changes how we view, plan for, and live in retirement.

> **The gospel not only changes our eternal destination, it also transforms our hearts and minds in the here and now.**

Figure 4 depicts this gospel-centered retirement. With the gospel at the center and all that it entails—faith, confession, repentance, conversion—its transforming power affects how we steward the time, talents, treasure, and our testimony of the gospel itself. Each of those areas is further expanded into other dimensions of the Christian life that are vital to living in retirement in a way that honors and glorifies God: character and perseverance, calling and vocation, stewardship and generosity, and serving and mentoring.

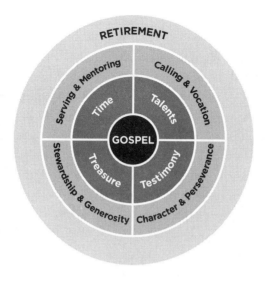

FIGURE 4: Retirement with the Gospel at the Center

Testimony: Character and Perseverance

The life-changing power of the gospel first and foremost results in a positional change between God and us. We are justified by grace, through faith in the substitutionary life, death, and resurrection of Christ; we have been declared righteous and are no longer subject to God's judgment and wrath against our sin (Rom. 5:1–11). None of the other effects of the gospel would be possible without this full reversal of our legal standing before God. Once made right with God, we cease to be haters and enemies of God and instead become his adopted children, calling him "Abba Father" (Rom. 8:15; Eph. 1:4–5). We are in a relationship with him; we love him, and he loves us, and our hearts overflow with gratitude for all he has done for us. We are now filled with God's Spirit, and we love, treasure, and worship God's Son, Jesus Christ.

Beyond this positional/relational change, the gospel progressively transforms every area of our lives as we believe and apply the it, allowing it, through the power of the Holy Spirit, to change our motivations, values, views, attitudes, and actions (Rom. 12:1–2). We continually press toward the goal of Christlikeness, although we will never fully achieve that in this life (1 John 3:2). This character change is to characterize the life of every believer as we put off the works of the flesh and put on the fruit of the Spirit (Gal. 5:19–23). In the context of retirement, as we put on the fruit of the Spirit, we will become the older men and women God has called us to be to our family, friends, church, and community.

We receive salvation at conversion, but living the Christian life requires an ongoing work of transforming and empowering grace. And remaining faithful to the gospel and its ongoing work in our lives is no easy thing. Life can be challenging, and getting older presents many difficulties of its own. In addition to diminished physical and mental capabilities, aging also presents character challenges. Of course, spiritual maturity and a life of godly character are important for everyone, not just those who are older. However, elaborating on Titus 2, commentator Matthew Henry wrote: "Old disciples of Christ must conduct themselves in every thing agreeable to the Christian doctrine." He goes on to say that "those who are full of years should be full of grace and goodness, the inner man renewing more and more as the outer decays. . . . Aged persons are apt to be peevish, fretful, and passionate; and therefore, need to be on their guard against such infirmities and temptations. Faith, love, and patience are three main Christian graces, and soundness in these is much of gospel perfection."[4]

The Bible urges us to persevere in spite of difficulties and trials (Heb. 10:36; James 1:2–3; Col. 1:11). This means we keep going in spite of obstacles and setbacks, seeking the sustaining power of the Holy Spirit each day so that we can stand firm in faith and press ahead against all opposition. In his second letter to Timothy, the apostle Paul compares the Christian life to a "fight" and a "race" that is to be finished and won (2 Tim. 4:6–8). For many, retirement is the final lap of that race, the "home stretch," if you will. Even if we don't retire near the normal retirement age of 65 or 66, most of us will likely live in retirement for many years, and preserving to the end is of the utmost importance. It is a race we must finish, but the victory has already been won for us by Christ.

Living and then finishing the Christian life well is something that all Christians should aspire to. It may be a race and a fight, but it is also a journey—one that takes us through different times and seasons. Once we have committed our lives to Christ, there should be no turning back. The author of Hebrews warns us to take care so that we "hold firmly until the end the reality that we had at the start" (3:14).

Perhaps you have known older people who, for whatever reasons, have become hard-hearted, detached, and disengaged. Falling away can take many forms. It doesn't just mean falling away from faithfulness and obedience toward God; it could also mean withdrawing, shrinking back, or retreating into self-centeredness, apathy, bitterness, cynicism, greed, or resentment. Such Christians will not enjoy the full, abundant life that God intends for them. In contrast, finishing the retirement race well means that we will make the most of whatever time we have left on this earth to fulfill God's calling on our lives using whatever gifts he gives us. With each passing moment, we are all getting closer to the day when our time on this earth will end; this gives us hope that the difficulties and challenges we will face as we age will be temporary and are merely to help us toward our final, eternal home.

Talents: Calling and Vocation

The Christian life is a "called life." First, we heard and responded to the gospel call. Beyond the gospel call—which is the entry door to salvation and life as a Christian if responded to by faith, belief, and confession of Jesus as Lord—there are other callings that we can glean from Scripture that pertain to how we should live our lives.[5] God calls us in his Word to be disciples of Jesus Christ, making the most of whatever talents, abilities, and resources he has given us for all the days of our lives and in whatever vocations, including those in the stage of life we call retirement.

Each of us has been given gifts in some measure—resources, time, talents, training, skills, and interests—which collectively comprise the potential we have to fulfill our individual calling. Fulfilling that calling is our own unique way of doing God's work by using what he has specifically given us in many different settings (home, work, church, and community). I would describe these as our *vocations*, which in this context refers to the multiple roles that each of us has as a spouse, parent, single person, church member, citizen, worker in those different spheres of life. In retirement, having been freed from the constraints of a paid vocational position, we have the opportunity to pursue new vocations. God may specifically call someone to leave a full-time, paid position and retire so that they can do something that he has preordained for them to do. Regardless of what these vocations are for each of us, we know God has good works planned for us, "which (he) prepared ahead of time for us to do" (Eph. 2:10).

Some of our gifts may diminish as we age, and, as a result, there will be things that we can no longer do, or do well. But in spite of that, we must determine not to shirk back from God's call in the later years of life to continue to live out our true identity in Christ as God's image-bearers and restorers. We must do all we can, with the grace that God provides, to remain involved with our families and in our neighborhoods, churches, and communities. Retirees too often withdraw from the mainstream of life instead of staying in the game and contributing.

There are a lot of ways that a Christian retiree can "stay in the game." Some things that come to mind are attending services, participating in men's and women's groups, praying, studying Scripture, giving generously, participating in a small group, going on mission trips, caring for the poor, loving our neighbors, sharing the gospel—the list is endless. These are most certainly among the good works God has called us to do, regardless of age or stage of life. We engage in these activities as best we are able throughout our lives as those who have been changed by God's grace through the gospel of Jesus Christ. But, if we think of good works only in these religious activities, we might miss the extent to which God's plan for our good works is much broader and deeper.

The Bible calls us not only to do good things, but to walk in the good works God has for us. The word *walk* is often used to refer to a way of living, a lifestyle. So, the good works we walk in are not just the obviously religious activities scattered throughout an otherwise secular life. Instead, the good works encompass the whole of the Christian and his/her life—all that we do by God's grace for God's purposes and for God's glory.

It's absolutely right and proper for us to invest ourselves in the life of our church and to engage in works of outreach for the sake of the poor, the oppressed, and those who don't know God's grace in Christ (perhaps even more so when we are more freed-up in retirement). But the Bible tells us to view our whole life as an interconnected series of good works—a living sacrifice—offered to God: "Whatever you do, in word or in deed, do everything in the name of the Lord Jesus, giving thanks to God the Father through him" (Col. 3:17).

Treasure: Stewardship and Generosity

Stewardship is rightly focused on our money and possessions. But these things are given to us by God as means to an end and not as ends in themselves. He knows that we need money to live, to provide for ourselves and our family whether we are retired or not; it is indispensable in meeting both our short- and long-term needs (1 Tim. 5:8). Stewardship in retirement means thinking about and planning for retirement when we are young and how we will fund it with the money God has given us when we are older. But stewardship is not just about budgets, or getting out of debt, or saving and investing wisely. There is also an important connection between stewardship and kingdom mission.

Christians are called to be missional, which is to share and model the gospel and to make disciples of Jesus Christ for the glory of God. After Jesus rose from the dead, he commanded his disciples to spread the gospel (Matt. 28:19–20). Some things can be done without money—we can share the gospel with our neighbor without spending a dime. But there is a connection between money and the broader mission of the church. As Jaime Munson wrote: "Mission doesn't happen without money, and money doesn't happen without a lot of planning, discipline, patience, reverse engineering, study, and cooperation. Work hard, make money, and use it as an instrument to glorify God."[6]

Through wise stewardship, we can free up money to give in the service of God's kingdom and the spread of the gospel. Money can, as Munson goes on to say, be used as a "prop on the stage of God's story, used or pursued for good or ill, to God's glory or our own destruction. . . . Through stewardship, we can . . . cultivate a heart of gratitude for the gifts that God has given, and righteously use those gifts to reflect the heart and priorities of Jesus."[7] I love his idea of money as a prop—something that God gives us to use as a part of his story of redemption; it is a straightforward yet compelling description of stewardship.

Our participation in gospel mission through generous giving shouldn't end because we are retired. Giving can be challenging in retirement because we don't know how much money we are going to need or for how long, but through careful planning and saving, we can seek to be useful to God with whatever we do have to give.

> **Through wise stewardship, we can free up money to give in the service of God's kingdom and the spread of the gospel.**

Generosity is something we should cultivate and grow in over our lifetime, but it will look different for each of us along the way. We have to do our part by endeavoring to practice biblical stewardship while continually trusting God for his gracious blessings and provision so that we can give generously throughout our lives. Ask the Lord to "make every grace overflow to you, so that in every way, always having everything you need, you may excel in every good work" (2 Cor. 9:8). Good works are an essential part of the Christian life, and good stewardship compels us to use whatever abundance God has given us to perform the good works that he has called us to do. That includes giving while in retirement and until the end of our lives.

Time: Serving and Mentoring

The gospel changes our hearts and our priorities and reorients our lives "God-ward" and "others-ward" instead of "self-ward." Because it causes us to love God and people, we structure our lives around our local church and gospel ministry in our city and beyond (Gal. 5:13). Jesus told us that whatever we most treasure will captivate our hearts; it will be what we most love and desire and give our lives to (Matt. 6:21). Because of the gospel, instead of treasuring riches, leisure, and worldly pleasures, we desire "to do what is good, to be rich in good works, to be generous and willing to share, storing up for treasure for [our]selves as a good foundation for the coming age, so that [we] may take hold of what is truly life" (1 Tim. 6:18–19).

Much has been written about finding and fulfilling one's life purpose in retirement. There are many paths a person can follow, but for those who have been changed by the gospel, our purpose is clear: we are called to invest ourselves in the lives of others, both inside and outside of the church, and to persevere in godly zeal as we grow old so that we can finish well to the glory of God (2 Tim. 4:7). If instead we retreat from a focus on God and the needs of others toward a self-centered life, as many retirees are prone to do, we will not fulfill Paul's command in Philippians 2:4 to: "look out not only for [our] own interests, but also for the interests of others." This is the essence of a life transformed by the power of the gospel—a life marked by godly character, faithful perseverance, clarity of profession, and generous giving of time, talents, testimony, and treasure for the furtherance of God's kingdom.

One of the most valuable ways that older Christians can serve is to mentor and disciple those who are younger. Younger Christians need older role models who can also be their friends. An inspiring relationship in the Bible is between Paul and Timothy. Some scholars believe that Timothy may have been in his teens when he and Paul first met, or probably no older than his early twenties. Paul adopts Timothy as a "son" in the faith. They are very different people, but they formed a personal and spiritual connection. Paul became his role model and his mentor, and Timothy became Paul's representative to the church in Ephesus to deal with several problem situations there.

I once read a good definition of a mentor: "Someone whose hindsight can be someone else's foresight."[8] Mentors are not just teachers; they are living examples whose life experience and wisdom can help younger people avoid poor judgments and bad choices, but most important, who can give them a vision of what it looks like to live for Christ throughout all seasons of life. The Christian life is not a philosophy or a religion; it is a way of life built upon and centered on the gospel, and the rich experience that an older mentor can provide can be priceless to a younger believer.

Even now, you can probably think of someone you could serve by giving them the benefit of the life experience and wisdom you have acquired over the years. An excellent place to start is with your children and grandchildren if you have them. You can also spend time with younger people in your church. My wife and I have the privilege of being a part of a small group in our church that has several young couples in it and also a few singles. It is a joy to be with them and share our lives with each other. I also recently got involved in a discipleship group for young men in support of the college ministry at my church. There are also opportunities in your community to get involved with children, young couples, and families. The main thing is to try to avoid spending all your time in a familiar, comfortable circle of same-aged peers. Look for opportunities to spend time with others who can benefit from your experience and wisdom (and don't forget you can benefit from spending time with them too!).

With more life experience, and hopefully the wisdom gained from it, older adults have wealth to share with others (Rom. 12:4–8). Fulfilling your calling in retirement work requires resisting fears of inadequacy or failure. Many retirees buy into the idea that they are too old to make an impact. For most, that is patently false. To discover what God has called you to do, start doing *something*—perhaps experimenting with different things to find your niche. The real question is not, "Should I be using my retirement to serve others in the context of my local church?" but, "How can I faithfully pursue the work God has for me to do in my church and beyond?"

Retirement Is a Gift from God

The majority of us will work most of our adult lives. If we are fortunate enough to reach a stage in later life when it is no longer a necessity for us to work full-time for a living, then we should be very grateful. It is a privilege that is mainly for those of us in developed nations—the rest of the world knows little of it. The potential freedom to leave a full-time job and pursue other personal interests, activities, and goals is a wonderful gift that should not be underappreciated. As Billy Graham wrote, "There isn't anything wrong with retiring, and those years can be some of the best of our lives if we can see them as a gift from God."[9] I would add, ". . . and live them accordingly."

=========================== Summary ===========================

- The transforming power of the gospel and the grace that it gives us throughout our lives is at the center of a God-honoring and glorifying retirement.

- As we steward the time, talents, treasure, and testimony that God has given us, we can fulfill our callings and vocations later in life by continuing to grow in character and perseverance, serving and mentoring, and stewardship and generosity.

- Each of us has to decide how we will live in retirement based on biblical principles and the specific things we are called and gifted by God to do, and especially in light of the gospel and the kingdom of God.

- Retirement should be viewed as a gift from God that can be a time for greater service to him and others.

For Reflection

- When you think of your life in retirement, do you put the glory of the gospel and your relationship with Jesus at the center?

- In what ways do in you need to grow in the area of stewardship of your time, talents, treasure, and testimony?

- Of all the focus areas listed (calling and vocation, serving and mentoring, stewardship and generosity, character and perseverance), which ones in particular do you believe God wants you to most focus on in retirement? Why?

- Are you starting to reimagine what your retirement would look like if you focus on these things? What do you need to start doing now to prepare to make it a reality?

Part Two

REIMAGINE YOUR PLAN FOR RETIREMENT

Chapter 4

PLANNING FOR A REIMAGINED RETIREMENT

"We buy things we don't need with money we don't have to impress people we don't like." —Dave Ramsey

"The most important thought that ever occupied my mind is that of my individual responsibility to God." —Daniel Webster

God's Providence and Our Responsibility

In the first few chapters, we looked at retirement from both a modern and biblical perspective and began to consider what a *reimagined retirement* might look like. We dismissed the modern-day idea of retirement as an endless vacation as inconsistent with biblical principles and values, but acknowledged the reality of some form of retirement for most people in our culture.

If retirement at some point is likely for the majority of us, wouldn't it be wise to plan for it? Or can we just trust God to providentially care for us in retirement whether we plan or not?

The answer lies in two truths that the Bible clearly teaches: God's providence and our responsibility. God's providence means that he provides for us. Jesus said, "Don't worry about your life, what you will eat or what you will drink; or about your body, what you will wear. . . . For the Gentiles eagerly seek all these things, and your heavenly Father knows that you need them. But seek first the kingdom of God and his righteousness, and all these things will be provided for you" (Matt. 6:25, 32–33). To paraphrase, "Don't worry about your retirement; God knows what you need, and he will provide for you." And one of the ways he provides for us is through the wisdom he has given us in his Word, which includes guidance on why and how to plan for the future.

At the same time, the Bible makes clear that we have the responsibility to work hard and to act wisely. Proverbs 24:33–34 says, "A little sleep, a little slumber, a little folding of the arms to rest, and your poverty will come like a robber, and your need, like a bandit." To paraphrase again, "Work hard, or you'll end up broke!"

Therefore, for the Christian, this is not an either/or decision. On the one hand, we are exhorted to trust in God's providence; on the other, we are instructed to "[diligently] plan" rather than be "reckless" or haphazard in our approach to the future (Prov. 21:5). We need to do both. That means planning and preparing for an uncertain future by stewarding our resources wisely during our working years, and also trusting God to guide us and provide for us as we faithfully live for him.

Plan by Creating Financial Margin

In his book *Master Your Money,* Ron Blue introduces the concept of financial margin. Referring to financial planning, he states, ". . . first of all, [our] long-term objectives [such as retirement] will probably require substantial financial resources; and second, that without receiving an inheritance or striking oil, the only way to reach your long-term objectives is to spend less than you earn over a long period of time. In other words, you must have a cash-flow margin every year."[1]

To create margin, Blue recommends sticking to a budget, paying off credit card and other short-term, high-interest debt, having an emergency fund to cover three to six months of expenses, saving a reasonable amount for future major purchases, retirement, and college, and then to increase giving.[2]

Maintaining margin requires living below our means and making wise lifestyle and spending choices based on biblical convictions. But this can be a big challenge, especially in our hyper-consumeristic and materialistic culture.

Because contentment can be so elusive, we are tempted to want more money and things, even after we have enough. Paul reminds us in 1 Timothy 6:6–8 that there is great gain in the pursuit of godliness with contentment. If we find our contentment in God, we will be less likely to look to the things of the world for our joy and satisfaction, which can help us keep our spending on nonnecessities in check. Jesus warned his disciples about materialism: "one's life is not in the abundance of his possessions" (Luke 12:15). The implication is that any attempt to find true happiness by the acquisition of more and more stuff will only result in disappointment, and our possessions certainly won't be the final true measure of the substance of our lives: "A good name is to be chosen over great wealth; favor is better than silver and gold" (Prov. 22:1).

CASE STUDY (PART 1): MIKE AND DEBBIE

At this point, we introduce a case study for a young married couple, whom we'll call "Mike and Debbie." We are going to follow them through their various life stages and apply some of the material in this book to their situation. Perhaps your family is similar, or you will see yourself in some of their circumstances. Some readers will have less income and savings than Mike and Debbie and some will have more; therefore, it is important to focus on the principles and practices being applied rather than the specific numbers.

Our couple represents a reasonably average, middle-class family. Mike is 27, a college graduate, and Debbie is 25; she is also college-educated. They currently have an annual income of $45,000. Mike is employed in a salaried position, and Debbie is looking for a job. They have no children but plan to start a family in the next few years. They have student loans totaling $35,000 that they would like to pay off quickly. But with apartment rent at $950 and some other debt (medical, car loan, and credit card) totaling $4,000, they are finding it difficult. They have a small emergency fund of $500 but as yet no retirement savings. They try to regularly give at least 5 to 10 percent of their income to their church but would like to give more.

Mike and Debbie don't currently have much financial margin in their lives, not because they have an extravagant lifestyle but due to the amount of debt they are carrying. Consequently, they have little room in their budget for saving—for either short- or long-term needs. Because Debbie is looking for a job, their situation will improve when she has some income, but a lot of it will need to go toward paying down their debt. Once they do, they will have greater margin, permitting them to save and give more. Retirement is the last thing on their minds right now, but it would be wise for them to start saving something now, when they are young, due to the dramatic impact it can have on their long-term saving success.

Expenses Matter

A thorough and detailed treatment of budgeting, spending, debt, and giving is not within the scope of this book, as the main focus is planning for retirement. Yet it is impossible to completely divorce our budgeting and spending decisions from our planning for retirement for a couple of reasons. First, they determine how much financial margin we will have for things like saving for emergencies, retirement, and giving. Second, they often determine the level and type of debt we are willing to take on, and debt can have a big impact on the margin equation.

As shown in Figure 5, there are basically three kinds of expenses: fixed, variable, and discretionary. I don't include giving with these categories as, for most of us, our ability to give is directly affected by our level of spending in these three areas.[3] Giving should ideally be from our "firstfruits" (Prov. 3:9–10 esv), but for many it is from whatever is left after other expenses. Our fixed costs, which include things like taxes, housing expenses, and debt payments, don't change much from month to month unless we make significant lifestyle changes. Variable expenses, such as food, clothing, and medical bills, are nondiscretionary, recurring expenses that vary based on our level of consumption. Discretionary expenses are for nonessentials that we can choose to spend on or not, and often include things like recreation and entertainment and personal blow money.

As the figure shows, *margin* is whatever surplus we have after our fixed, variable, and discretionary expenses to save and give. This is not meant to imply that saving and giving are a lower priority than our other expenses; in fact, they should be the highest. But for many, due to an expensive lifestyle and the debt that so often accompanies it, financial margin is reduced, which impacts the potential level of saving and giving. There is a direct relationship between how much we spend and how much we can give and save. Obviously, the greater our financial margin, the more flexibility we will have with our saving and giving. We will also be better able to weather the inevitable economic storms that come our way.

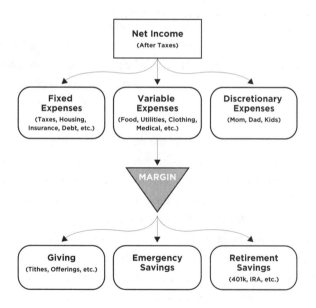

Fixed expenses tend to be the largest of the three. One of the main reasons so many people have little or no financial margin is because their fixed monthly costs are too high. If fixed monthly expenses are greater than 50 percent of after-tax income, then housing or transportation, or both, are the likely culprits. (Of course, in some areas of the country, housing expenses are off-the-charts and finding affordable housing can be pretty tough, even if you are okay with a smaller place.) Some may have hemmed themselves in by overcommitting to a bunch of monthly payments on everything from car loans or leases to cellular plans to Internet and cable.

Some Specific Recommendations

There are some particular things that can be done to create or increase financial margin. These will help with both short- and long-term financial goals, but the primary focus is on increasing retirement readiness.

"Smooth" your consumption

Most people experience what is called diminishing marginal returns when it comes to the amount of joy and satisfaction for each extra dollar they spend, and would, therefore, benefit from keeping their spending relatively flat. Looking back at Figure 5, keeping your total expenses (excluding your tithe and savings) at 75 percent or less of your net income, or perhaps getting it down to 70 or even 60 percent, will give you more and more margin in terms of discretionary dollars for giving and saving, especially as your income increases. The idea is to keep your spending at basically the same level or to reduce it as your income rises, which is known as consumption smoothing. (The opposite is also true. Someone who earns a high income can use consumption smoothing to help ensure that they have more stable and predictable levels of consumption should their income decrease.) Someone who spends 80 to 90 percent of their income or higher will stay trapped in a never-ending cycle of working and spending and will never think they have enough.

> **Key Concept:** *Consumption smoothing* refers to a way of optimizing your personal financial situation by keeping your spending level about the same each year. Overspending comes at the expense of saving and giving, which could mean that your overall standard of living when retired will be less than optimal.

The additional margin you gain will be available to save and give, and once your savings goals are met, you will be free to give radically. Those with lower incomes (at the poverty level, working poor, and most of the lower middle class) may always have to spend exactly what they earn—they are living paycheck to paycheck, so they will have little or no margin. Middle to upper-middle income earners have more spending flexibility, but they tend to have similar problems. They tend to increase spending commensurate with income, and as their confidence in future earnings tends to rise, they incur additional expenses based on the assumption of increased income in the future. In other words, they spend all they earn and then some. This is presumptive, which as we know, is unwise. One way to combat this tendency is to establish some spending limits.

Set spending limits

We are a spending society. In 2017, Americans spent well over 130 trillion dollars. Spending is not bad; in fact, it's one of the ways we make good use of the money we receive. Spending converts money into consumable goods and services that we can all use with a thankful heart (1 Tim. 4:1–5; 6:8; Matt. 11:19). We need to provide food, clothing, shelter, and transportation for ourselves and our families—what Dave Ramsey calls the "Four Walls" (see 1 Thess. 4:11; 1 Tim. 5:8). So God clearly wants us to enjoy the wonderful things he has put on the earth for us to develop and use (Gen. 1:28; 1 Tim. 6:17).

So our problem isn't that we spend, it's that so many of us spend everything we earn and sometimes more, which results in a lack of financial margin. Setting a spending limit to increase margin is simply a self-imposed cap on spending that enables consumption smoothing. Those with lower to middle incomes may be limited in their ability to institute such limits as, for all practical purposes, their spending is already capped by their income. If they exceed it, they would have to take on debt (usually with credit cards). But higher-income families can decide to spend no more than "X" percent per year no matter how much their income increases. To hold to the limit, they would need to track and manage their expenditures and resist the temptation to dramatically upgrade their homes, cars, and vacations simply because their income has increased.

In Table 1, I illustrate what this might look like for families at different income levels. Because I firmly believe that everyone should give some amount in proportion to how God has blessed them and how they feel led in their hearts, I have included a giving percentage in every income category, increasing the percentage as income grows (see 1 Cor. 9:7). Fixed expenses are higher at lower income levels because of the disproportionately higher percentage of income needed for things like housing and transportation. Spending for fixed and variable expenses as a percentage of income stays relatively stable at the $75,000 level and up, but to further increase margin, it could be a fixed amount rather than a percentage. For example, someone making $150,000 per year could cap their fixed expenses at $45,000 (45 percent of the $100,000 level), which would be $15,000 less than 40 percent of the $150,000 level ($60,000). The difference will create additional margin that could then be used for additional giving or saving or both.

INCOME	$25,000	$50,000	$75,000	$100,000	$150,000
Giving	5%	7.5%	10%	15%	25%
Spending Fixed	70%	60%	50%	45%	40%
Spending Variable	15%	15%	20%	20%	15%
Spending Discretionary	2.5%	5%	5%	7.5%	7.5%
Saving Short Term	2.5%	5%	5%	2.5%	2.5%
Saving Long Term	5%	7.5%	10%	10%	10%
Total	100%	100%	100%	100%	100%

TABLE 1: Suggested Spending Percentages by Income Level

It's important to keep an eye on spending in key categories in order to keep to a budget, especially those that tend to increase as one's income rises (housing, transportation, entertainment, vacations).

CASE STUDY (PART 2): MIKE AND DEBBIE

At their current income level of $45,000 a year, Mike and Debbie would use the $50,000 column in Table 1 as a guide, perhaps with some slight adjustments. Their rent is relatively appropriate for their income. But their fixed expenses may be more than 60 percent, depending on the amount of money they allocate to loan pay off. Furthermore, the need to take care of their debt makes any significant allocation to long-term (retirement) savings unfeasible at this time. They do need to add to their emergency fund (currently $500) to get it to at least $1,000, and $1,500 or $2,000 would be even better. Even with whatever additional income Debbie brings in, they will need to keep their expenses in check to create the margin they will need to pay off their debts and to be able to save and give more.

Focus on keeping fixed expenses in check

There are a few categories of fixed expenses which, if kept in check, deliver the most "bang for the buck" regarding holding to a spending limit. The most significant are housing and transportation because they tend to be the most substantial part of families' budgets.

As discussed earlier, keeping your fixed expenses at 50 percent or less of net income is one of the best ways to create margin. I also recommend capping your total mortgage expense (principle, interest, taxes, insurance) at 28 percent since this is an area where there is such great temptation to overspend.[4]

It's not uncommon to think about purchasing a "move up" house after you have been in your first house for 10 or 15 years. But remember, if you buy a more expensive house and don't pay cash for it, you are going to restart the mortgage loan payoff process again (heavily front-end loaded with interest expense), and you may eliminate all or part of the margin you have and end up spending the next couple of decades under greater financial pressure. A wise approach is to put a lot of money down and finance it with a 10- or 15-year mortgage, which will reduce interest costs and accelerate principal payoff, perhaps providing you with a paid-for home by the time you retire.

As you get close to retirement, you may start thinking about downsizing. Perhaps you want to reduce expenses, move closer to children, enjoy a change of climate, simplify your lifestyle, generate some retirement income from the sale of your principal residence, or move to a smaller and easier-to-manage property. Or you may decide to stay right where you are—in fact, most do. No matter what, it usually makes sense to enter retirement with a paid-for house and then to tap the equity later on for future needs such as health care or long-term care expenses if required. But keep an eye on ongoing expenses—if they are too high, consider moving into a lower maintenance/insurance/utilities/tax cost situation.

You can also cap your transportation expenses. According to Edmunds.com, the average monthly payment on a new vehicle is $479. That is a significant amount of money: $5,748 per year, to be exact. And that doesn't include taxes and insurance, which are higher on new cars. Also, according to the US government, transportation is the second-largest expense for most households after housing, averaging approximately 25 percent of take-home pay. That includes gas and maintenance, which can cost more for older vehicles.

CASE STUDY (PART 3): MIKE AND DEBBIE

It's now a year later, and Debbie has gotten a job making $30,000 a year. Consequently, their combined annual income is now $75,000. This has enabled them to build their emergency fund (to $1,500) and to accelerate their progress on paying off their student loans and other debts using the "debt snowball" approach. They have been in their apartment for several years now and are thinking about purchasing a house, but they know it will take a while to save up for the down payment once their debts are paid off. (They're shooting for 20 percent, which would get them the best terms and they can avoid paying for Private Mortgage Insurance [PMI].)

Mike's employer offers a 401(k) retirement plan and matches 100 percent of employee contributions up to 5 percent. Mike has started participating in his plan but is only contributing 3 percent (for a total of 6%) so that he and Debbie can continue to focus on paying off their debts. Debbie's company offers a similar plan, but she isn't signing up right away. Once their debts are paid off, they both plan to contribute at least enough to get the full employer match.

They are driving two older vehicles, and one of them is on its last leg. So, they have started saving in a "car replacement fund." That will slow down some of their payments toward their debt, but it will help ensure that they won't have to take on additional debt when the old car finally goes to car heaven.

The best way to keep your automobile expenses in check is not to buy new cars, especially if you have to borrow money to do so. The biggest reason for buying a used vehicle is to avoid the oversized depreciation in the first year of its life, much of which occurs just as soon as you drive off the car lot. Edmunds.com reports that a new car loses 11 percent of its value the instant you drive it away; other sources say it's closer to 20 percent with subsequent annual depreciation of 10 to 20 percent a year. A good used car that is three or four years old will have already lost 40 to 60 percent of its value, but that has been absorbed by the original owner. You can drive a decent vehicle at a fraction of its initial cost and, depending on the car and how well it has been maintained, it may have five or ten more years of good use ahead of it.

The bottom-line impact on your margin for retirement planning is pretty apparent: money not going to pay for a new car and car payments can be saved and invested for retirement, or used for other purposes. Think of it this way: if you are spending 32 percent of your net income on housing and 25 percent on transportation, you will only have 43 percent left for everything else! If you wanted to tithe 10 percent and save 10 percent, you would be left with only 23 percent to cover all of your other living expenses. So, like buying too much house, buying more car than you can afford can also cause big problems with cash flow and margin.

Avoid unnecessary debt

Most of us remember the trials and tribulations of the Great Recession that worked its way through the United States and Europe in 2007–2009. That financial crisis demonstrated once again just how precarious debt-based finances can be, both personally and globally. But now, at this writing ten years later, it's remarkable how little the financial crisis changed our relationship to debt and savings. Debt sharply declined between 2008 and 2013 as consumers sought to de-leverage, but has risen dramatically ever since. Ultra-low interest rates and better economic times are driving a lot of it, but we apparently haven't learned our lesson about the dangers of excessive borrowing.

Fortunately, the Bible isn't silent about debt. There obviously weren't Visa cards or auto loans in Jesus' time, but lending and borrowing were very much a part of the economic landscape. The Bible does not strictly prohibit debt, but it does characterize debt as a form of bondage. When we borrow, we become a "slave to the lender" (Prov. 22:7). And in the context of financial margin and saving for retirement, debt comes at another cost—the money that goes to creditors can't be used for anything else. That is the opportunity cost of debt. It can also cut into our financial margin, which reduces our flexibility to save and give.

> **Key Concept:** *Opportunity cost* is merely the set of choices and associated benefits that are missed when you choose one use of your money over another.

Based on this concept, there is an opportunity cost for every dollar that we spend. Therefore, we should seriously and prayerfully consider the eternal opportunity cost of everything we spend on ourselves that could have been used for other purposes. Any money that we spend on ourselves is not laid up in heaven (Matt. 6:20). That does not mean that we can *never* spend anything on ourselves; but it does mean that we should avoid materialism, covetousness, and unhealthy comparisons with others, which lead to self-indulgent overspending.

Another big problem with debt is that so many are hindered by it. In the past decade, overall US household debt has increased by 11 percent. Today, the average household with credit card debt has balances totaling $16,061, and the average family with any kind of debt owes $132,529, including mortgages.[5] Of course, this isn't always due to overspending. It is sometimes because of job loss, medical debt, and other unexpected events. This is important because there is a direct correlation between overspending with too much debt and a low savings rate. And as debt has increased, the savings rate in the United States has dropped to 2.4 percent, the lowest level since the debt-fueled hysteria of the mid-2000s. The disproportionate levels of debt and savings are concerning, especially as it relates to readiness for retirement.

Debt can be an even bigger problem for those who are close to or are in retirement. Most people, understandably, focus mainly on the income side of things—how to save enough before retirement and then generate enough income to pay the bills later on. This is important, but equally (or perhaps more so) is keeping expenses down as you enter retirement, especially if your income is limited.

Getting rid of debt is one of the best ways to reduce expenses. So, if you are still working, now is the time to pay off debt, while you are bringing home a paycheck—regardless of which stage of life you're in. If you are younger, work to pay off debt to free up money to help you save and give more. If you are older, do it for the same reasons, and to better position yourself for retirement, as it may be tougher when you are retired, and you wouldn't want to use your tax-advantaged retirement savings to pay it off if you don't have to.

Use a budget to track and manage expenses

A budget is basically a spending plan—a written, predetermined approach to the use of our income based on the categories and limitations we have established. Dave Ramsey says: "A budget is telling your money where to go instead of wondering where it went. . . . Give every dollar a name. Every dollar has a destination."[6] It's not a backward-looking tracking of our expenses—that is record-keeping. A budget first looks ahead toward what we plan to spend and then looks back by tracking what we actually spent. Only then can we determine whether we are hitting our giving, spending, and saving targets.

A good approach is to create a budget before the start of the month. Start with some basic categories and percentages based on the spending categories that work for you. If someone is experiencing financial distress, there are two basic categories: "above the line" and "below the line" expenses. The key differentiator is between absolute necessities (food, clothing, shelter, and transportation) and everything else. But for everyday budgeting, there are five major expense categories: savings, fixed expenses, variable expenses, discretionary expenses, and giving. They can be broken down in a variety of expense categories. You can refer back to Table 1 to see how to best break down these expenses according to your income.

When preparing a spending plan, keep it simple but no more so than it needs to be; you want to be sure you are tracking things at the right level of detail. It's best to prepare a zero-based budget, which means that after you're finished, your projected income minus your planned outgo should equal zero. Every dollar has to have an intended destination![7]

Tracking and managing your spending *before* retirement will help you better plan and save for when you are *in* retirement. In the next chapter, we're going to get into the all-important topic of saving.

Summary

- God has promised to provide for his children, but he also gives us wisdom and instruction on what we need to do to steward his resources well.

- Planning and preparing for retirement begins as soon as we get our first paycheck. Our lifestyle and spending decisions before retirement will determine how much financial margin we will have for giving and saving, and whether we will have enough in retirement.

- Although Scripture doesn't specifically prohibit debt, excessive debt, or the wrong kind, can be a hindrance to achieving our stewardship goals.

- It is important to consider the opportunity cost of the money we spend, especially the eternal opportunity cost.

- Setting up a budget for managing and tracking our spending is a great help.

For Reflection

- Do you expect God to provide for you in retirement regardless of what you are or are not doing for yourself? If so, how would you define *provide*?

- Are you living at, above, or below your means? If you are spending more than you earn, what is causing it? What can you do to change that?

- If debt is a big problem for you, do you have a plan to eliminate it, especially if it is hindering your giving and saving?

- Do you deliberately consider the opportunity cost of the money you spend, especially to service debt or on nonnecessities? How can you be more eternally focused in your spending and giving?

Chapter 5

SAVING FOR RETIREMENT

"The lesson of the rich fool [in Luke 12] is not 'don't save.' In fact, the Bible offers numerous guidelines for how to save for the future in a way that honors God. . . . Save as an act of prudence and stewardship, not as an act of anxiety and fear of what the future may hold." —Jaime Munson

"All of us can learn good stewardship by enacting the following: Spend Less than You Earn, Give Generously, Avoid Debt, Plan for Financial Margin, and Set Long-Term Goals." —Ron Blue

Saving is an area where many Christians get confused and feel conflicted. We want to handle our resources in a way that honors and obeys the Lord, but sometimes it can be difficult to know how to best align our spending and giving—and especially saving—with biblical teaching. When it comes to specifics in this area, the Bible is long on principles and short on practices. It doesn't tell us exactly how much to spend or save each month, and there is no one-size-fits-all approach. This is why understanding, embracing, and adhering to the stewardship principle and the vast amount of wisdom the Bible provides on this topic is so important.

The Wisdom of Saving

Spending and giving are both good uses of the money that God gives us, but so is wisely setting money aside for needs that we know we are going to have in the future. Proverbs 6:6–8 directs us to examine the ant so that we may "observe its ways and become wise . . . it prepares its provisions in summer; it gathers its food during harvest." Yet some Christians wonder if they should save much of anything, since the Bible has so much to say about the dangers of hoarding and greed and with so many immediate needs around them.

Not surprisingly, the Bible addresses both saving (but not out of fear or greed) and generosity (to those in need). Not spending everything but also saving for an uncertain future, which would include a time when you can no longer work (due to age, weakness, sickness, loss of job), or because you no longer want to work for pay and instead volunteer your time to serve God and others, is wise (Prov. 21:20). Deciding not to save (or to save very little) and then assuming that God or others will take care of us no matter what is presumptive toward God, and we are told, "Do not test the LORD [our] God" (Deut. 6:16) in terms of our future provision. We are also instructed to "honor the LORD with [our] possessions and with the first produce of [our] entire harvest" (Prov. 3:9), which instructs us to make giving a priority over saving. But wisely saving provides for a surplus that can be used to "[have] something to share with anyone in need" (Eph. 4:28). Such resources may enable you to respond faster and possibly in a more impactful way than if you did not have them. If you have a surplus, it makes it much easier to give "when it is in your power, [not to] withhold good from the one to whom it belongs" (Prov. 3:27). Savings may also provide you with something to leave behind in the form of a financial legacy.

Saving is also one of the ways to fulfill our family obligations (1 Tim. 5:8). There are some circumstances (particularly death or illness when income may be reduced or cease) in which our dependents can be provided for through savings or insurance.[1] (That is not to exclude the assistance of family and friends, but we should not presume on that.) If I were to die at the age of 70 and my wife lives to age 90, I want to do what I can to ensure that she is provided for during the last 20 years of her life. For us, that would be through Social Security survivor benefits and savings. That doesn't mean that my wife would never need help from anyone, I just want to do all I can to ensure that she is cared for. If I don't do that, I could impose a burden on our children, other relatives, the church, or the government.

The Dangers of Saving

Many things are good for us, but in excess can be dangerous (food, for example). Savings is a good way to prepare for the future, but if we aren't careful, it can increasingly become the target of our heart's affections and displace God as the primary source of our hope and security.

The Bible emphatically states that it is impossible to divide our affections between God and money: "No one can serve two masters, since either he will hate one and love the other, or he will be devoted to one and despise the other. You cannot serve both God and money" (Matt. 6:24). So if on the one hand, it is advisable to set enough money aside and to invest it wisely to meet our anticipated needs in retirement, and on the other, we are warned not to put our faith and hope in our savings, how can we reconcile these seemingly contradictory perspectives?

The solution lies in the fact that the Bible uses the words *foolish* and *fool* to describe the extremes on both ends of the saving continuum.

It can be foolish to save nothing or too little, especially if we know we will have needs in the future, as the funds won't be there when they're needed. But on the other extreme, saving can become hoarding, which is also foolishness. Ecclesiastes 5:12 says, "the abundance of the rich permits him no sleep." Why? Maybe because of anxiety and fear that he will lose his wealth or that he does not have enough. Verse 13 goes on to say: "There is a sickening tragedy I have seen under the sun: wealth kept by its owner to his harm." The hoarder saves more than necessary and then holds on tight because his faith and trust is in his wealth rather than God. This is foolish because the hoarder is acting as an owner, not a steward.

> The Bible uses the words *foolish* and *fool* to describe the extremes on both ends of the saving continuum.

We have to recognize that wealth in the form of savings can be a blessing or a stumbling block, but because of our sinful tendencies, it is sometimes the latter. If God enables us to save, and we do so consistently and wisely, we could end up with a pretty good-sized nest egg. Therefore, we must guard our hearts and not put more trust in our savings than we do in God. They can't provide true peace and happiness—only God can. So, the key is to hold our savings loosely and not to trust them to deliver what they never were intended to.

As the apostle Paul told Timothy: "Instruct those who are rich in the present age not to be arrogant or to set their hope on the uncertainty of wealth, but on God, who richly provides us with all things to enjoy. Instruct them to do what is good, to be rich in good works, to be generous and willing to share, storing up treasure for themselves as a good foundation for the coming age, so that they may take hold of what is truly life" (1 Tim. 6:17–19).

When to Start

You probably already know the answer: the sooner, the better. This can't be emphasized enough.

There's not much sense talking about how to allocate, invest, and take income from your savings in retirement if you don't have anything saved. And there is cause for concern; generally speaking, we are spenders, not savers. According to an authoritative study, the average saved for those age 56 to 61 is $161,577. Now, that may sound to you like a lot of money—but it isn't if you have to withdraw 4 to 5 percent or more a year to live on in retirement. Social Security will provide some help, but the average benefit from that program is around $1,300 per month ($15,600 per year), which may not be enough for many people.[2]

CASE STUDY (PART 4): MIKE AND DEBBIE

We fast-forward three years. Mike is now 31, and Debbie is 29. Their combined income has increased to $78,000/year, and they are about halfway toward paying off their outstanding debts. Even though their loans aren't paid off yet, Mike and Debbie decided that they want to increase their saving for retirement. So Mike has raised his contribution from 3 percent to 5 percent, and Debbie has started saving 3 percent of her income. Since both of their employers match 100 percent, up to 5 percent of compensation, they are now effectively saving a total of 16 percent of their gross income (5% + 5% + 3% +3%), which is good since they got started a little late. That equates to $12,480 per year. Both are pre-tax defined contribution plans, which gives them additional margin as they can reduce their withholding for federal income tax.

They have also increased their giving to 10 percent of their pre-tax income, which is greater than the 8 percent of their money that they are contributing to their retirement accounts. Plus, they are continuing to save for a car and have also started saving a little each month toward a down payment for a house. The key for our couple at this stage is to keep the right level of focus on retiring their debt since they have diverted some of that money to save in their 401(k), saving for a car and a house down payment, and increased giving. They are hoping to have a child very soon, so that will have financial implications as well. They will need to continue to hold the line on their living expenses to maintain the financial margin they have worked so hard to create.

Most experts recommend saving at least 10 to 15 percent for retirement, and starting as soon as possible. If you're 28 years old and in your first real job, the last thing on your mind is saving for retirement. After all, it may be 30 or 40 or more years away. But before you dismiss the idea altogether, consider this: when you're in your 20s, you can start investing relatively little, and if you do it consistently for the rest of your life, wind up with a lot more money than someone who invests the same amount but starts ten years later.[3] If you think that's just some financial mumbo jumbo, take a look at Figure 6. If Bob begins saving for retirement at age 25, putting away $5,000 a year for 40 years, he'll have around $774,000, assuming earnings grow at 6 percent annually. Now, let's say, Bethany, who is also 25, waits just ten years until she's 35 to start saving. She puts away the same $5,000 a year for 30 years, and her earnings grow at the same 6 percent a year. When she's 65, she'll wind up with around $395,000—*less than half* the money that

Bob will have at the same age. Bethany would have to save a LOT more money each year just to get close, which she may not be able to do.

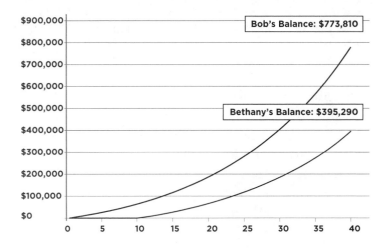

FIGURE 6: Benefit of Early Saving

Seems like a no-brainer, doesn't it? It should be. Save a little now and reap the benefits later. But unfortunately, many of today's youngest workers pass on the opportunity to save for retirement early, when the beauty of compounding interest, which Albert Einstein called "the eighth wonder of the world," can work its "magic" and maximize savings. Time is what causes the blessings of compound interest and tax deferral to really do its thing—money starts to grow itself.

Key Concept: *Compounding* is simply the ability to reinvest the earnings from an investment which, in turn, generate their own earnings that can also be reinvested. Over a long period of time, compounding has a positive snowball effect.

It is hard to get precise numbers about the saving habits of young adults. In a 2019 paper from the Brookings Institute Economics Study Program, the authors state that millennials (those born between 1981 and 1996), "accumulated less wealth than most previous generations at the same age," and that "median wealth among Millennials in 2016 was lower than among similarly aged cohorts in any year from 1989 to 2007."[4] This suggests that young adults are starting out further down the savings curve than the Gen Xers or the Baby Boomers who preceded them.[5]

Another report published in 2018 by the National Institute of Retirement Security, which was based on 2014 data, reported that nearly two-thirds of working Millennials have not saved anything for retirement. And though two-thirds of them have access to an employer-sponsored retirement plan, only one-third contribute to it.[6]

The implication of this isn't just that younger workers are saving less and have a lower net worth that their predecessors did—it's that they have less money invested at a time in their lives when the long-term effects of compounding can have their greatest impact.

Where to Save

If you decide that you want to save, you need to put your money somewhere, assuming you don't put it in your mattress or bury it in a can in your backyard. (Both of which I would highly discourage.) The optimal choice is to fund savings retirement accounts that allow you to contribute either pre-tax or after-tax so that your savings can grow tax-deferred until you withdraw them; or, in case of Roth accounts, have tax-free withdrawals. Some plans, such as the 401(k) and 403(b), are specific to employers. Others, such as an IRA and Simple IRA, are for individuals. Figure 7 shows these various before-tax accounts and whether an after-tax (Roth) option exists:

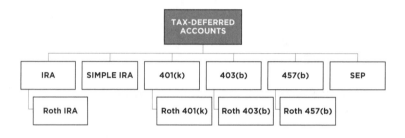

FIGURE 7: Types of Tax-Deferred Retirement Accounts

Defined Contribution Plans: 401(k) and 403(b) (Traditional and Roth)

An employer's defined contribution plan will be the best option for most retirement savers. These are retirement accounts that allow pre-tax contributions (up to a certain amount each year) in traditional accounts, and after-tax in Roth accounts, but both grow tax-free until the funds are withdrawn in retirement. Traditional accounts are taxable upon withdrawal, but the Roth is not, which is the main reason that many people prefer the Roth if it is available to them.

These accounts usually have another significant advantage: employer matching contributions. The matching percentage will vary by employer, but typically companies match from 50 percent all the way up to 100 percent of an employee's contribution up to a certain percentage of their gross salary. For example, if you save 5 percent, and your employer matches 100 percent of your contributions up to 5 percent, you are effectively saving 10 percent; that can really accelerate your savings.

Limited investment choices and administrative costs can be a concern in employer plans, but they are funded through payroll deduction, so your savings are on autopilot. An added benefit is that regular investing results in what is known as dollar cost averaging. As you save regularly using automated mechanisms, you will invest at different cost points. Over time, this tends to work in your favor as you invest at market highs as well as lows.

Individual Retirement Arrangements (IRAs): Traditional and Roth

These accounts are similar to 401(k)-type accounts because contributions also grow tax-deferred. The big difference is that they are self-administered—not set up and managed by employers. You can save for retirement in an IRA if you don't have an employer-sponsored defined contribution plan, but many people add to these accounts after they have contributed the maximum to their employer's plan. But if your employer matches 100 percent of your income up to 5 percent, you are effectively saving 10 percent, and there is no need to contribute to an IRA unless you want to save more.

There are two types of IRAs: Traditional and Roth. The main difference is in the way they are treated for income tax purposes when you contribute and then withdraw, and also required minimum distributions (RMDs) at age 70.

Table 2 shows some of the key distinctions between Traditional and Roth IRA accounts (as of 2019):

TRADITIONAL IRA	ROTH IRA
1. Contributions are tax-deductible within certain income levels up to certain limits 2. Most distributions before age 59½ will incur penalties 3. Forced distributions (known as "RMDs") start at age 70½ 4. Distributions are taxable as ordinary income when you take them, including gains made in the account	1. Contributions aren't tax deductible 2. "Qualified" distributions/ withdrawals are not taxable— account must be open for five years to qualify 3. Earnings are taxable and subject to an early withdrawal penalty only when withdrawal is not a "qualified" distribution 4. Single filers need to have below $122,000 gross income to fully contribute; married limits are higher (less than $193,000 for a full contribution) 5. Graduated contributions are allowed: single filers—at least $122,000 but less than $137,000; married filing jointly—at least $193,000 but less than $203,000 6. No RMDs

TABLE 2: Traditional versus Roth IRAs (2019)

You can contribute to a Traditional 401(k) or IRA up to the annual limits as long as you have enough income. However, there are income limits based on your modified adjusted gross income (MAGI) that determine whether you can contribute to a Roth account or not. If you can't contribute to a Roth account, your option is to contribute to a traditional (pre-tax) 401(k) or IRA.

One of the main arguments for the Roth IRA is the widespread belief that tax rates will go up and be significantly higher by the time you are in retirement. All other things being equal, taxes will probably increase, at least for the wealthy. But for most, the tax rate in retirement has gone down, because a retiree's income is usually significantly reduced. And seriously, if your income isn't diminished in retirement, taxes may be the least of your worries anyway.

Simplified Employee Pension IRA (SEP) and Savings Incentive Match Plan for Employees (SIMPLE) IRA

SEPs are used by those who are self-employed for their tax benefits and because they offer higher annual contribution limits than regular IRAs. Contribution percentages can vary, but in 2019 the annual limit was 25 percent of compensation up to a maximum of $56,000. The SEP can be used by business owners who have employees and want to make contributions on their behalf, similar to a 401(k).

SIMPLE IRAs are similar to SEPs, but they are established by employers—including self-employed persons, sole proprietorships, and partnerships—for their employers. Employers must make either matching contributions up to 3 percent, similar to 401(k)s, or non-elective contributions which are paid to eligible employees whether they contribute or not.

Deferred Income Annuities

Annuities allow your savings to grow tax-deferred without being in an IRA or another retirement plan. This makes them a good option for savings that you want to shelter from income taxes after you have maxed-out your regular 401(k) and IRA retirement accounts, or if you don't have access to them for some reason. Deferred Annuities are generally complex and high-cost and should be carefully evaluated before you put any money in them. They are most attractive to more wealthy individuals due to their tax-deferred status.

Brokerage Accounts

A brokerage account is typically used to purchase various types of investments, such as stocks, bond, mutual funds, and Exchange Traded Funds (ETFs). They can be used in retirement and nonretirement accounts. Some financial services companies don't require a brokerage account to buy their funds directly. Most brokerage firms charge a commission for buying and selling certain types of securities, but those costs have been steadily decreasing.

Allocating Your Savings in Retirement Accounts

Let's assume that your goal is to save 10 percent of your pre-tax income of $75,000 annually. You can use an employer 401(k) and an IRA to allocate your savings optimally between these accounts.

Maximize the employer's match in your 401(k). The first place that you should put your retirement savings dollars to work is in your employer's 401(k) to maximize your employer's matching contribution. Assuming your company matches 50 cents on the dollar up to 5 percent of gross income (which essentially equates to 50% of 5% or 2.5%), if you contribute the maximum of 5 percent, or $3,750, you will effectively be saving 7.5 percent of your income ($5,625). You are already well on your way to your target savings of 10 percent ($7,500)!

Contribute to your IRA. Even if you contribute to a 401(k), you can also save in your IRA up to the annual limit allowed by the IRS, which in 2019 was $6,000. In this case, in order to reach your annual savings goal of $7,500, you need only to save an additional $1,875 (2.5%) in your IRA.[7]

This simple allocation strategy is summarized on the next page in Table 3.

ALLOCATION TYPE	ALLOCATION AMOUNT	BALANCE
10% Savings Target	$7,500	$7,500
5% to 401(k)	($3,750)	$3,750
2.5% from 401(k) Employer Match	($1,875)	$1,875
2.5% in IRA	($1,875)	0

TABLE 3: Simple Allocation Strategy

Need to save more? If you decide that you need to save more than 10 percent, you have some options: First, you could contribute more to your IRA, up to the maximum of $6,000 (as of 2019). Then, you could contribute more to your employer 401(k) up to the $19,000 maximum under current 2019 rules, *or* you could open and/or contribute to a spousal IRA and contribute up to the maximum of $6,000 in it. Both options would give you the ability to save more than 10 percent, and if necessary, much more.

How Much Is Enough?

Your projected expenses in retirement are the key driver of how much you will need to have saved. Most experts believe that retired couples in the United States can live on anywhere from $2,500 to as much as $10,000 per month. The former will support a very frugal lifestyle whereas the latter will fund a much more lavish retirement, but most will fall somewhere in between and want to maintain a spending level that is roughly comparable to their preretirement lifestyle. That may or may not be attainable based on a variety of factors, the most important being your saving rate relative to your income and spending in preretirement.

In addition to their projected expenses, any estimation of how much someone will need to have saved for retirement to supplement Social Security and other guaranteed income requires the assumption of an annual withdrawal from savings in some percentage (or amount). A widely used strategy is what is known as the 4 percent rule, which has also been called the safe withdrawal rate or sustainable withdrawal rate based on work by Certified Financial Planner William Bengen.[8] After running many computer simulations, Bergen found that a constant amount of spending from a diversified stock and bond portfolio of approximately 4 percent would have been "safe" (safe meaning the portfolio was not completely depleted) in 95 percent of historical 30-year stock market return periods. More recently, as economic conditions have changed, another noted researcher, Dr. Wade Pfau, found that the safe withdrawal rate is now closer to the 3 to 3.5 percent range.[9] There is also growing sentiment among retirement planning professionals that more dynamic strategies are needed that account for changes in market returns (they could be less than historical trends), life expectancy (which can change due to health conditions and other factors), and other unknowns. I will discuss some of these alternative strategies in chapter 8, which deals with income distribution strategies in retirement.

Table 4 shows the estimated amounts you would need to have saved based on a 4 percent annual withdrawal rate to supplement different levels of Social Security and/or pension benefits to generate a particular level of retirement income.[10] For example, if you earn $80,000 preretirement and need $60,000 in retirement, and your estimated Social Security benefits will be $25,000 per year, you will need to have $875,000 saved. If you can live on less or don't have a long life expectancy, you can get by with less.

DESIRED ANNUAL INCOME	SOCIAL SECURITY AND/OR PENSION	ESTIMATED AMOUNT SAVED @ 4% WITHDRAWAL RATE
	$15,000	$625,000
$40,000	$25,000	$375,000
	$40,000	$0
	$15,000	$1,125,000
$60,000	$25,000	$875,000
	$40,000	$500,000
	$15,000	$1,625,000
$80,000	$25,000	$1,375,000
	$40,000	$1,000,050
	$15,000	$2,125,000
$100,000	$25,000	$1,875,000
	$40,000	$1,500,000
	$15,000	$2,625,000
$120,000	$25,000	$2,375,000
	$40,000	$2,000,000

TABLE 4: Required Savings Estimates (Based on 4% Withdrawal Rate)

If you'd like to get an idea of whether you're on track with your savings based on your current age, I used a retirement planning tool on the Fidelity Investments website to construct the chart shown in Table 5.[11] Most people will retire in their 60s, but I included estimates for age 70 as some will want (or need) to work longer. (The multipliers for retiring at age 70 are in parentheses.) As an example, if you are age 40 and earning $75,000 per year, you should have 3 times your pre-tax income, or $225,000, saved for retirement. If you want to retire at age

67, you will need $750,000 at that time. If you plan to wait until age 70 to retire, you should have $150,000 at age 40 and $600,000 by the time you hit 70. You need less money saved at age 70 because you are starting withdrawals later and your savings won't have to last as long.

SAVINGS REQUIRED AT AGE...										
25	30	35	40	45	50	55	62	65	67	(70)

Current Age | Checkpoint (x current pre-tax income)

Current Age	25	30	35	40	45	50	55	62	65	67	(70)
25	--	1x (1x)	2x (1x)	3x (2x)	4x (3x)	6x (4x)	7x (5x)	8x (6x)	10x (7x)	11x (8x)	(8x)
30	--	1 (1x)	1X (1x)	2x (2x)	3x (2x)	4x (3x)	6x (4x)	7x (5x)	8x (6x)	10x (7x)	(8x)
35	--	--	2x (1x)	2x (2x)	3x (2x)	4x (3x)	6x (4x)	7x (5x)	8x (6x)	10x (7x)	(8x)
40	--	--	--	3x (2x)	3x (2x)	4x (3x)	6x (4x)	7x (5x)	8x (6x)	10x (7x)	(8x)
45	--	--	--	--	4x (3x)	4x (3x)	6x (4x)	7x (5x)	8x (6x)	10x (7x)	(8x)
50	--	--	--	--	--	6x (4x)	6x (4x)	7x (5x)	8x (6x)	10x (7x)	(8x)
55	--	--	--	--	--	--	7x (5x)	7x (5x)	8x (6x)	10x (7x)	(8x)

TABLE 5: Estimated Savings Required by Age

The Fidelity tool makes a variety of assumptions to come up with these estimates. They mainly have to do with an estimated income replacement of 45 percent of preretirement income, excluding Social Security and any pension income for retirees with average total expenses in retirement. That amount, when combined with Social Security, would provide approximately 70 percent of their preretirement income. If you think that Social Security won't be around when you retire (and it may not be, at least not in its current form), then you will need to increase the multiplier, perhaps double it. If you think your expenses will be much higher, maybe due to inflation, you may want to adjust for that as well.

CASE STUDY (PART 5): MIKE AND DEBBIE

Mike and Debbie are now 35 and 33, respectively. They have had their first child, but are still living in their two-bedroom apartment. (They are continuing to save for a house and are about three-fourths finished with paying off their student loans.) Debbie stopped working to be home with the baby, who is now three years old, but her employer allowed her to return to work part-time from home. She is currently earning $14,000 a year. Unfortunately, as a part-time employee, she can no longer contribute to her 401(k), but she or Mike can open and contribute to a Roth IRA instead. Mike has received a couple of raises and a promotion and is now earning $60,000 a year; therefore, their combined income is now $74,000/year, which is slightly less than what they were earning before the baby. He and Debbie have been saving in their retirement accounts for quite a few years now (Mike since he was 28 and Debbie since she was 29). Their total savings balance, including employer contributions and earnings, is $55,000. (Their investments are 80 percent stocks and 20 percent bonds, and profits have averaged 9 percent a year.) Let's take a check-point to see how they are doing.

According to Table 5, if they want to retire at age 67, they should have approximately two times their current annual salary (or $148,000) saved for retirement. At $55,000, they are behind, mainly due to a late start, but they are still young and time is on their side. Plus, with Mike's recent promotion, their combined income is almost back to what it was before Debbie went part-time. Just the same, they may want to consider ramping up their savings to a total of 20 percent, including employer contributions. To do that, Mike would need to increase his savings to 15 percent, which he could do by opening a Roth IRA and contributing 5 percent of his income to it each year (he is already contributing 10 percent to his employer savings plan, including the 5 percent match). The additional 5 percent ($3,700) would go into Debbie's Roth IRA. On the other hand, if they plan to work at least until age 70 (many will), they are closer to the recommended target for their age (which is one times salary, or $74,000).

The challenge for Mike and Debbie is where to find the additional $3,700 per year ($308/month) to save in the IRA. They don't want to stop paying off their student loans since they're almost done or reduce their monthly giving, so they will have to find it somewhere else. The only place to look is to find ways to reduce their other monthly expenses.

Those who start earlier may be able to save less, whereas those who begin later will need to set aside more. And keep in mind that some portion of that may come from an employer match in your 401(k)/403(b)-type plan. If your employer matches 100 percent up to 3 percent in your 401(k), and you contribute 6 percent, you will effectively be contributing 9 percent. Remember, this is not an exact science; we can't accurately predict what our future needs will be because we don't know all the factors that will be in place when that time comes. You may be able to live on much less than what the model assumes or your expenses could be much higher.

What if You're Behind?

If you did a checkup for your situation using either of the tables above, there are some things you can do, but be careful not to over-react—whether you have concluded you have saved too little or more than enough.

Don't get too focused on "your number"

The simple formulas and tables that we have looked at can leave us with the idea that it's all about "a number." They assume that you can know "the number," and that if you reach "the number" you will have no concerns in retirement. The math is important, but it shouldn't have the final word. There is no way to know what will happen in the future—whether the markets will be good or bad, or how long you will live, or how much money you will need to spend 15 years from now. So, what looks mathematically sound now may not hold up in the long run.

My recommendation is to use the numbers as a guide but realize that there is a fair amount of uncertainty and there may need to be adjustments along the way. Furthermore, many of these formulas are built on a vision of retirement that we said earlier is inconsistent with biblical principles. That being said, if you think you are way off course in your saving, there are some steps you can take.

You may need to start saving more

If you're participating in a 401(k)-type plan, save at least enough to get the matching contribution. Then you could start (or increase) contributing to an IRA. And remember: both spouses can have an IRA even if only one of them has an earned income. If you're playing catch-up, you should probably have a savings target of at least 15 to 20 percent of your gross income. For those ages 50 and older, take advantage of the saving *catch-up provision* for retirement accounts. As of 2019, a worker age 50 or older can save an additional $6,000 in a 401(k) account and catch-up IRAs contributions can be increased by $1,000.[12] And remember, these provisions apply to both spouses. If you can't find the money to save, then try to find ways to reduce your expenses to create greater margin.

Consider working longer and retiring later

This may not be what you had in mind, but it may be just what you need to do. And, as we say in Table 5, it can make a significant difference in how much you need to have saved. Your savings will continue to grow (even more now that you hopefully have more to grow than you have in the past), as will the amount you will receive from Social Security. (The difference in the amount you will receive at age 70 versus age 62 could be as high as 76 percent! That could make a big difference over the long haul.)

A Final Word about Saving

At the beginning of this chapter, we looked at the wisdom and the danger of saving. If you save and apply the other wise principles I discuss in this book, you should have enough to retire when the time comes. And once you start saving, you want your money to grow. If it idly sits in a cash account, you will lose money due to inflation. In the next chapter, we will look at the importance of wisely investing the resources God has entrusted to you so that you can help them to grow while being careful not to take more risk than you are comfortable with. In chapter 8, we will look at the role that savings play in generating some of the money you need to live on in retirement.

Summary

- Saving is condoned in Scripture as a wise way to meet both short-term and long-term needs.

- We should not save at the expense of giving, and as our savings accumulate, we must guard our hearts so that we do not begin to place our faith and trust in them instead of God.

- The sooner we start saving for retirement the better, even if it's a small amount. The power of compounding will cause our savings to grow over long periods of time.

- The decision on how much we need to save—the amount needed for retirement—is an important one that will vary based on our individual situation.

- Consider setting a savings finish line so that your resources can be freed up for other purposes.

- If you are behind in retirement, don't lose heart. You can trust God for your provision while doing all you can to play catch-up.

For Reflection

- Do you struggle in finding the right balance in your life between spending, giving, and saving?

- Are you saving something for retirement, even if it's just a little? If not, what steps can you take now to free up something to save?

- Do you have a savings target—a finish line? If so, are you on track to meet it?

Chapter 6

INVESTING FOR RETIREMENT

"The individual investor should act consistently as an investor and not as a speculator." —Ben Graham

"October: This is one of the peculiarly dangerous months to speculate in stocks. The others are July, January, September, April, November, May, March, June, December, August, and February." —Mark Twain

Investing in a retirement context is typically done in two major phases: the *accumulation* phase (before retirement) and the *distribution* phase (in retirement). These are stage-of-life related, so timing will vary by individual. The *accumulation* phase is the time leading up to retirement when the focus is on saving up and investing with asset growth as the main goal. The *distribution* phase comes later when we are in retirement and are living off our savings along with other sources of income such as Social Security and perhaps a pension. There is a shift from a focus on growth to income and also the preservation of capital; in other words, gaining becomes less important than not losing. However, some amount of growth to offset inflation should also be part of the investing picture in retirement.

The Wisdom of Investing

The Bible doesn't tell us exactly how much to spend, give, or save; nor does it tell us exactly how we should invest. As Wayne Grudem wrote, "There are different ways in which we can save [or invest, which in this context refers to holding cash, bank deposits, stocks, and bonds], all of which are morally acceptable at least to some extent, and none of which in themselves are morally wrong."[1] Ron Blue, referring to the purpose of investing, said: "Investing is simply taking a reasonable risk to reap a future reward. . . .The scriptural justification for investing is to multiply assets to meet future *needs* [author's emphasis] for you or others."[2]

The biblical model for investing is based on stewardship, which includes making wise investing decisions with accountability to God for the resources he gives us to manage. One of the main lessons from the Parable of the Talents in Matthew 25 is not so much that the servant squandered his master's money, but that he was lazy and did not take an opportunity to do something productive with it. Because of that, his master called him an "evil, lazy servant," and said: "you should have deposited my money with the bankers, and I would have received my money back with interest when I returned" (Matt. 25:26–27). Clearly, the master expected the servant to do more than just "stuff it in a mattress." In the same way, God expects us to prudently put the resources he gives us to productive uses.

I should take a moment here to note that investing is an area of personal liberty. Though, as I've shown, I believe the Bible gives us good reason to feel confident in investing humbly and wisely, you may have a different conclusion. If it violates your conscience to invest, that is okay—don't do it! You can even skip this chapter and move on to the next, if you like. But, because I think it is wise and biblically permissible to invest (with some guardrails), I will continue to advocate for such.

All investing involves some reasonable risk-taking, but unlike burying it in the backyard or gambling in the casino, when we invest wisely in accordance with biblical principles, we are putting the money to some constructive use. A key differentiator of different investment alternatives is the risk that you will lose money, which is balanced against the potential reward (how much money you could make). Your sensitivity to this risk is called your risk tolerance.

> **Key Concept:** *Risk tolerance* is the amount of swing you can tolerate in the value of your investments. Risk tolerance is an important factor in making investment decisions because if you take on more risk (to get higher returns) than you can tolerate, you might overreact and sell at the wrong time.

But perhaps you wonder if you should invest at all, especially in stocks, and whether it would be better to keep the money safely stashed away in a Federal Deposit Insurance Corporation (FDIC)-insured bank deposit account somewhere. Some caution about investing in stocks is warranted; stocks can be risky, and although investing in stocks isn't prohibited by Scripture, there is a clear distinction in the Bible between investing (equity ownership of successful companies that deliver products and services) and gambling (which is highly speculative risk-taking).[3] When it comes to investing in businesses by buying stocks, the Bible seems to sanction some risk-taking and profit-sharing if done wisely (Prov. 31:10–31; Eccles. 11:1–6). People have historically purchased interests in business ventures, with the associated costs and risk, with the goal of sharing in the profits. But as we know all too well, gain from such investments is uncertain and should not be presumed.

The Dangers of Investing

Investing is like a minefield—there are wise paths to travel, but a major misstep can lead to ruin. If you want to avoid all danger, don't invest. But that decision has its risks—you won't grow your money, and it will be eaten up by inflation. A lot of the risk associated with investing is macroeconomic and market-related, and our tendency is to react to it in sometimes emotional and irrational ways. But other dangers have more to do with our hearts than our heads.

One of the greatest dangers is greed. Greed is merely a desire for more than what we need. Closely related to greed is envy or covetousness—when we want for ourselves the blessings that others have received. These temptations can lead to falling prey to "get rich quick" schemes that may ultimately lead to disaster. Proverbs 28:19–20 goes as far as to say that someone who "chases fantasies will have his fill of poverty," and a person who is "in a hurry to get rich will not go unpunished." The sad consequences of chasing after easy wealth could be financial ruin. Those overcome by a gambling addiction know this all too well.

Pride is another danger in investing. Successful investors can be tempted to want recognition, admiration, and respect for their accomplishments. First Timothy 6:17 warns the wealthy about becoming arrogant, and Proverbs 16:18 plainly says: "Pride comes before destruction, and an arrogant spirit before a fall." Have you noticed how eager your friend or relative is to tell you about the brilliant stock/option/bitcoin/or whatever investment they made and just sold it for a big profit? What about all the times when they lost money; why don't they mention them? The reason is pride.

The temptations of greed, envy/covetousness, and pride can cause us to be overconfident or desperate and take undue risks, such as when we bet on an overly risky stock or another opportunity offering an oversized return based on the low-probability occurrence of some event in the future. This risk isn't measured and calculated—it is speculative and presumptive, two attitudes condemned in Scripture. The Bible teaches us to be wise and humble in our attitude toward ourselves and the future and not to be overconfident of either.

How to Invest

With awareness of the dangers of investing and humility of heart, we may decide to invest. These are some basic steps we can take to do so in a way that is consistent with our stage-of-life, goals, and risk tolerance:

1. Understand your investment options and choices

Before we do anything else, we first need to understand the various asset types, their characteristics, and relative risks. This will help us to decide which assets we want to hold in our investment portfolios. We will look at four basic types, although there are several variants in each.

Cash and Cash Equivalents: These include cash (in a mattress), checking accounts, money market accounts, certificates of deposit (CDs), and similar types of investments which are essentially cash. Some may come with FDIC insurance (currently up to $250,000 per insured account). Generally, any money you invest in cash or a checking account will have a zero rate of return or negative return due to inflation. Savings accounts, money market accounts, and CDs usually pay a bit more. But given the low yields and inflation risk of cash, you may want to look elsewhere for better options, especially when investing long-term for retirement.

Bonds: Investing in bonds is a way of loaning money to businesses or governments. You can buy bonds with varying returns based on term, assigned risk, and market interest rates when they are issued. Yields are currently relatively low (for short- and immediate-term bonds, in 2 to 5% range), but can go much higher during periods of high interest rates. Company bonds are viewed as riskier than government bonds, mainly because of the higher risk of default. Bonds also have interest-rate risk. When rates go up, bond prices go down since a bond's current yield isn't as attractive to investors as newer issues that pay more interest. The longer the term, the higher the interest paid to bondholders, but also the greater the interest-rate risk. Bonds are considered safer than stocks, which is why so many people diversify their stock holdings with bonds. But because of default and interest-rate risk, they are by no means absolutely safe. In fact, some types of bonds (such as junk bonds) are as risky as certain types of stocks, at times even more so.

Company Stock: When you buy a stock, you own a part of a company. This is called purchasing equity. Stock ownership is a productive use of our investment capital, as it helps companies employ people and provide goods and services. It also entitles you to a share of the company's returns based on their profit and earnings (dividends) distribution policy. However, such gains are not guaranteed and can vary from year to year. Some companies stop paying dividends altogether during times of economic stress.

The companies themselves, and therefore their stock, are categorized by the total value of the company's capitalization—"Large," "Mid," or "Small-Cap." Capitalization is calculated as simply the number of shares times the price per share. These companies can be US or foreign companies. Foreign companies can also be classified based on market cap size, as well as whether they are in developed or emerging markets. Larger, stable companies (called blue chips) that have a history of paying dividends are considered less risky than newer, highly leveraged companies, such as start-ups. Domestic companies are usually less risky than international ones, with emerging market businesses being the riskiest. Stocks are viewed as riskier than bonds because, if the company fails, investors could lose all the money they have invested in it.

Alternative Investments: These include a variety of things including Real Estate Investment Trusts (REITs), Master Limited Partnerships (MLPs), hedge funds, options, and even more exotic things to speculate in such as land, precious metals, and commodities. Some of these, such as precious metals, may help insure against inflation and economic breakdown, but tend to be highly speculative due to their high volatility. Holding some of these provides diversification, but holding too much can tend toward hoarding, as the money isn't being put to productive use. Notice the fear motivation behind many of the ads you see for buying gold on TV.

2. Unless you're an expert in stocks and bonds (or are willing to pay someone who is), invest mainly in Mutual Funds and/or Exchange Traded Funds (ETFs)

You can own individual stocks and bonds. They can be purchased for a commission in a brokerage account. However, market timing and stock picking can be pretty risky unless you are a highly skilled financial analyst. Mutual Funds or ETFs are a better alternative for most. Mutual Funds are collections of individual investments made up of some combination of the assets listed above, usually with a desired target investment area, such as an industry (e.g., technology) or a class of investments (e.g., municipal bonds or large-cap stocks) and sold on a per-share basis. ETFs are similar, but differ in that they can be bought and sold on an exchange in real time like an individual stock. Both are baskets of securities, typically holding assets of the same type (stocks, bonds, or real estate), but some differentiate further based on asset class—for example, mid-cap stocks versus large-cap stocks or short-term bonds versus long-term bonds.

3. Decide between actively managed versus passively managed funds

Most mutual funds are actively managed—the fund managers select and time buying and selling of positions to maximize return. Their goal is to do better than their market benchmarks. Some managers do, but most do not, as outperforming the markets at large is hard. More than 80 percent of active fund managers don't regularly beat their market benchmarks. There are actively managed funds in virtually all asset categories, and the management fees they charge can vary significantly, usually in the .5 to 1.5 percent range. Many actively managed funds also charge an up-front sales charge (called a load).

Active fund management has advantages, especially for certain types of funds in particular market conditions. Active fund proponents believe that the financial markets aren't always efficient, that they don't set the price for stocks and bonds perfectly, that active managers can leverage those inefficiencies by finding discounted securities that deliver better long-term returns. The strategy is to hold more of the investments that they think will do better instead of those best aligned with a particular benchmark. Active fund managers rely on in-depth research and analysis on the companies they buy, which help them identify investments they believe will outperform the market. Some also practice "market timing" to "buy low and sell high" to further optimize gains.

Passive management is typically associated with low-cost index funds, so called because they track the performance of their respective market indices. These index funds are composed of stocks or bonds that partially or fully represent a specific market index. The goal of passive management is not to beat the market but to take whatever the market delivers at a lower cost than actively managed funds.

> **Key Concept:** A *market index* is a weighted average of many stocks or other investment vehicles from a particular sector of the financial market, and it is calculated using the price of the selected securities. Market indexes are used to track an entire stock or bond market, or some part of it.

For example, the Vanguard 500 Index Fund fully represents the S&P 500 Market Index, which is comprised of the 500 largest companies in the United States. There are also passive mutual funds—Vanguard, Fidelity, Schwab, and others all offer them. ETFs are usually passively managed, but more actively managed EFTs are coming on the scene. ETFs are known for their low cost (typically .05 to 1.0%) and no up-front sales charges. However, because they trade like stocks, there may be a greater temptation to buy and sell at the wrong times. Some financial professionals suggest that the average investor does not need ETFs for just that reason. Others like the low cost, holdings transparency, and trading flexibility.

Table 6 shows some of the key differences between actively managed and passively managed funds:

KEY FEATURE	ACTIVE MANAGEMENT	PASSIVE MANAGEMENT
Management Fees	Generally higher than passive	Generally lower than active
Tax Efficiency	Depends on the investment manager (varies by fund)	Generally tax efficient
Potential for Above-Market Returns	Yes	No
Potential for Below-Market Returns	Yes	Yes, after incorporating fees
Decision-Making Process	Seeks to capitalize on market conditions	Seeks to replicate the performance of the funds benchmark

TABLE 6: Active versus Passive Management

Actively managed funds still have more assets under management, but investor interest and investments in passively managed funds are increasing. One reason is that, at a minimum, they virtually guarantee market-based returns. Plus, the management fees tend to be higher for actively managed funds, and they can add up over an extended period. In contrast, most passive index funds have very low fees, and some zero-cost funds are now available.[4]

4. Decide whether to hire an investment advisor or do it yourself

Many people are "do-it-yourselfers" (DIY) by default as they are already choosing the investments in their 401(k) or 403(b) accounts and perhaps also in an IRA. But some investors want to use the services of a financial advisor, especially as they get closer to retirement and roll money from an employer-sponsored plan to an IRA. These assets have to be well-managed for several decades and missteps during that time can have serious negative repercussions. Both approaches have their advantages and drawbacks—the right option for you depends on your situation.

A professional advisor can help construct and manage a portfolio that is right for you, relieving you of that burden and the stress that comes with it. This is the wise thing for most people. If you go that route, it would be preferable to hire one that is not paid on commission and, therefore, less prone to conflicts of interest. The problem with commission-based compensation structures is that they motivate (through financial incentives) financial sales people to make sales transactions, and moreover, to focus their sales activities on high-commission financial products. This is natural. It isn't the fault of the salesperson (most are honest and trustworthy); it is a problem within the financial services industry itself. In my opinion, commissioned sales have the greatest conflict of interest because the incentives for the broker may not be aligned with your interests and can even be diametrically opposed. Plus, commissions and fees are on top of the expenses associated with the investments themselves, and this can all really add up and detract from your earnings.

If you want to hire an advisor, look for a Registered Investment Advisor (RIA) designation. These are advisors who operate under client fiduciary rules and are not paid commissions on the specific investments they recommend to clients. Instead, they charge fee-for-service or fee as a percentage of assets-under-management. Ask your advisor for full transparency and disclosure of every way he and/or his firm make money off the money you invest with them, and make sure that they don't exclude anything, no matter how small it is. Also make sure you not only get information on the management fees but also for the investments themselves. This is another problem with the industry—costs are often undisclosed or obfuscated via layers of complex paperwork and jargon that *you* have the responsibility to read, but most people don't.

One of the best things about having a trusted advisor is what they do to help you keep a steady hand on the wheel, especially when things get tough (and they will). They can also be a big help with income planning during the distribution phase of retirement. But if you go the DIY route, you're taking full responsibility for selecting your investments and managing the portfolio. Your costs will probably be lower than an advisor-managed portfolio, but you will still have to pay the management fees for the investments you choose.

Your investment options as a DIY investor are almost endless. The most straightforward DIY approach is to purchase a single fund, such as a Target Date Retirement Fund. You could use this in your 401(k) (if available), your IRA, or both. With this approach, you would purchase a fund based on your age and desired retirement date. As you get closer to retirement, the fund automatically adjusts its asset allocation across various stock and bond sub-funds—from more to less aggressive based on the percentage allocated to stocks. Your other options include constructing a simple portfolio of low-cost index funds covering the major asset classes listed in Table 7: Morningstar Risk Allocation Model in accordance with your age and risk tolerance, which we discuss in Number 5 below. Anyone interested in going the DIY route needs to take the time to get educated on investing basics. Most important, they will need the discipline to stick to their investing strategy when the going gets tough.

5. Minimize risk and maximize returns through diversification and asset allocation

When choosing investments, we always have to decide between less risk, lower returns, and more risk, higher returns. Diversifying our investments, and then choosing the right allocation of them within our portfolio, is one of the most important decisions you will make.

In Ecclesiastes 11:2, the Bible presents this concept in a context that isn't completely clear, yet seems to suggest a wise approach to maritime commerce or simply spreading one's resources around due to the uncertainties of life: "Give a portion to seven or even to eight, for you don't know what disaster may happen on earth." This uncertainty is echoed in James 4:14 where we read: "Yet you do not know what tomorrow will bring—what your life will be! For you are like vapor that appears for a little while, then vanishes." Both verses acknowledge the normal ups and downs of life that can impact our finances, and diversification is one way to inject a margin of safety into our portfolios.

> **Key Concepts:** *Asset Allocation* and *Diversification.* Asset allocation is the percentage of your portfolio invested in different asset classes, such as stocks, bonds, and cash. It determines the overall level of risk in your portfolio. Diversification goes further and spreads your investments across the various asset classes to balance risk across and within these classes to, hopefully, offset each other and therefore prevent significant losses.

The keys to managing the risk/return allocation that suits you best are your age and risk tolerance. When you are young you can afford to take more risk because you know that even if the market tanks, it will probably come back to new highs within 12 to 24 months. Retirees, on the other hand, usually want to ratchet down their risk and, although most would love to have a portfolio with big returns but minimal risk, that generally isn't feasible except in high-interest-rate environments. Investors need to diversify with low-risk/low-return and high-risk/

high-return investments based on their age and risk tolerance. Figure 8 shows the relative risk/reward (return) for the major asset categories we looked at earlier. As you move up the curve, you are taking additional risk to increase the likelihood of making more money. Remember, there is *no* guarantee this will happen—you could make more, but you could also lose a lot.

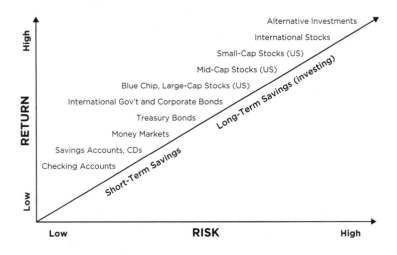

FIGURE 8: Investment Risk Continuum

Table 7, which is taken from the Morningstar Target Risk Allocation,[5] provides a suggested allocation model based on different risk profiles, from conservative (which might be the posture of later-stage retirees) to aggressive growth (which may be more typical of those just starting out).

ASSET CLASS	AGGRESSIVE	GROWTH	MODERATE	BALANCED	CONSERV-ATIVE
Domestic Equities	59.00%	49.00%	37.00%	26.00%	13.00%
International Equities	36.00%	31.00%	23.00%	14.00%	7.00%
Domestic Fixed Income	4.00%	18.00%	33.00%	49.00%	63%
Foreign Fixed Income	1.00%	2.00%	4.00%	6.00%	10.00%
Alternatives	0.00%	0.00%	2.00%	4.00%	5.00%
Cash	0.00%	0.00%	1.00%	1.00%	2.00%
Total	100%	100%	100%	100%	100%

TABLE 7: Morningstar Risk Allocation Model

Which model you gravitate toward will be determined by two main factors: your age (and investing horizon) and risk tolerance. Table 8 shows different investing strategies based on your life stage and corresponding risk tolerance. For example, if you are a 40-year-old who is at least 20 or 30 years from retirement, you may want to consider a growth-oriented allocation, whereas those nearing or in retirement would be more income-focused with less emphasis on growth.

INVESTING STAGE (AGE)			
	Starting Out (25–34)	Investing Diligently (35–44)	More Focused on Retirement (45–59)	Early Retirement or In Retirement (60+)
OBJECTIVE	Income, Saving	Grow income, Saving, Investing	Retirement saving, Investing	Retirement income and capital preservation
TIME HORIZON	Long (25+ years)	Long (15–25 years)	Medium (5–15 years)	Short (< 5 years)
RISK TOLERANCE	High	Medium–High	Low–Medium	Low
ALLOCATION CATEGORY	Aggressive to Growth	Growth to Moderate	Moderate to Balanced	Conservative

TABLE 8: Investing Strategies by Age

Table 9 shows how major asset classes behave differently in various economic scenarios and how at times they off-set each other:

ASSET CLASS	RETURN	GROWTH	RECESSION	INFLATION	DEFLATION
Domestic Stocks	10%	up	down	up	down
International Stocks	9%	up	down	up	down
Bonds	5%	up	flat	down	up
Real Estate	3%	up	down	up	down
Gold (Commodities)	3%	flat	down	up	down
Cash	<1%	flat	flat	down	up

TABLE 9: Asset Class Behavior in Different Economic Scenarios

During times of inflation, US stocks generally do well (growth is up, earnings increase; therefore, share prices rise); however, although bond *yields* may be higher, prices will fall. One of the ways you can prepare for these different scenarios is to make sure you allocate across the various asset classes and that you adequately diversify within the classes based on your risk tolerance. If you invest in international stocks, you wouldn't want to allocate everything to emerging markets; you'd want to diversify across developed and undeveloped markets to mitigate risk. Similarly, you wouldn't necessarily put your entire bonds investment in intermediate-term corporate bonds; you may want to include some US Treasury bonds as well for added safety. But be aware that you will likely have to exchange the potential for higher returns in return for less volatility. If you invest too heavily in bonds, you expose yourself to inflation risk; an increase in interest rates or inflation will reduce the value of your investments, and you'll lose money with them as well.

Key Concept: *Inflation risk* is the threat that rising prices for goods and services will reduce the value of the dollar and, therefore, some of the value of the growth in your investments, and reduce their purchasing power when you are spending them later on.

With stagflation (lower inflation and slower growth), stocks and bonds will both be crimped. We need to look no further than the housing bust of 2008–2010 to remember that real estate can lose value as well.

It is important to maintain your allocation strategy over time, meaning that you will need to occasionally rebalance your portfolio to bring it back to your target allocation. One of the most common ways of doing this is by simply selling assets that have done well and purchasing more of those that haven't.

Key Concept: *Portfolio rebalancing* is as process whereby we adjust the relative weight of the assets within a portfolio, typically by buying or selling assets in order to bring particular asset classes back to the original target allocation percentage.

Once you retire, you will probably stop adding to your savings and will begin spending from them instead. If you experience significant losses during that time, it can be tough to recover. The financial markets tend to trend in cycles, and some downtrends can last a very long time, limiting your ability to recover from significant losses. This is known as sequence of returns risk.

Key Concept: *Sequence of returns risk* is the risk that you retire during an unfortunate period of poor market returns. It has a "double whammy" effect in that your savings balance goes down in value at the same time you start taking money out, further reducing your portfolio.

The main variables of sequence risk are whether there are poor investment returns in the early years of retirement, how bad they are, and the duration. The lower the performance and/or the longer the period of a market decline during the early years of retirement, the greater the risk that you will outlive your money in the long term. In contrast, if returns are generally good during the first half of retirement, some bad years toward the end may be irrelevant since you will probably have enough to live on at that time.

6. Keep an eye on fees and costs, monitor your progress, and stay the course

Some investments are costlier than others, so try to keep fund expenses as low as possible. This is especially important for long-term investors as they can really add up over time. That's because fees reduce returns on an annual basis. (A portfolio that earns 6 percent but pays out 2 percent in fees will only earn 4 percent.) Plus, that 2 percent is no longer able to compound over the next 10, 20, or 30 years, which would have ended up being a pretty big number.

Actively managed mutual funds tend to have higher fees than passive funds and ETFs. If you choose mutual funds, look for no-load funds with low management fees. You may not be able to eliminate all costs from investing, but you can minimize them, and that helps maximize long-term returns.

If you invest wisely, you won't need to be checking the markets and your account balance every day. If you do, you'll be tempted to start tinkering with it. Reviewing it once a quarter, and possibly rebalancing once a year, should suffice. Resist the temptation to react every time something happens in the markets.

CASE STUDY (PART 6): MIKE AND DEBBIE

It has been awhile since we checked in with Mike and Debbie, and there have been a lot of changes in their lives. They are now officially in middle-age, as Mike is 43 and Debbie is 41. They have three children and live in a house they purchased a few years ago for $178,000 with a $142,000, 30-year mortgage. The house has appreciated some and is now valued at $185,000. They finally paid off their student loans but still have a few thousand in outstanding credit card and medical debts. They are working to pay them off.

Our couple has been consistent in their saving and giving. Debbie is still working from home part-time, and her earnings have increased to $18,000/year. God has continued to bless Mike in his career, and with raises and bonuses he is now making $72,000/year, so they now have a combined income of $90,000. However, Debbie plans to stop working in a year or two so that she has more time to spend with her children, volunteer at their school, and participate more in church-related activities. When she does, their income will fall to $72,000. Because they were conservative in their house purchase, their monthly house payment Mortgage Loan Calculator (PITI) of $875.00 will still only be about 24 percent of their take-home pay, so they will be able to maintain some margin.

Based on their ages and Table 8, Mike and Debbie are in the "Investing Diligently" phase (age 35–44). They are continuing to save 20 percent of their income (including employer contributions) in Mike's 401(k) and a Roth IRA. They still have a long-term retirement planning horizon and are comfortable taking a moderate to high amount of risk with their investments. They have chosen to maintain their 80/20 allocation between stocks and bonds, which according to Table 8 (Morningstar's recommended asset allocation by age), is a growth-oriented portfolio and appropriate for their age and time horizon. They will probably maintain that for at least the next ten to fifteen years. At that point, they may want to ratchet back the stock allocation to 60 percent or 70 percent.

Their total retirement savings have reached $326,000. Looking back at Table 5 in chapter 5, they should have about four times (4x) their annual income saved ($288,000, once

($288,000, once Debbie has stopped working), so they are now a little ahead. This is good, as they may need to reduce their savings plan contributions percentage just a bit, perhaps to 15 percent, since their income will be reduced when Debbie stops working.

Avoid Perfectionism

No matter what you do, you will never have a perfect portfolio. If you are always pursuing one, you will be tempted to continually tinker with your investments, which will likely be to your detriment since investors often buy and sell at the wrong times. Because the financial markets and the economy, in general, are unpredictable and can at times behave in erratic and irrational ways, there is no such thing as a perfect investment strategy. Therefore, the "perfect" portfolio is the one that is best for you based on its cost, management approach, and risk profile. Risk is perhaps the most critical component. If you take little or no risk, your savings may not grow enough to offset inflation. If you take too much, especially when you are close to or in retirement, you may experience significant losses at a time when you can least afford them. No magical allocation will protect us from all the risks of investing—including stuffing it all in your mattress, as you will be assuming significant inflation risk! Each of us has his/her own view of where the most significant risks exist, and your investment decisions should be based on limiting exposure to the most significant risks in your situation.

We have seen how wise investing is another good way of stewarding the money that God has entrusted us with and an essential part of a plan for retirement. If we start saving early and invest wisely based on our age, goals, and risk tolerance, we will put ourselves in a better position to retire when the time comes. In addition to our retirement savings, there are some other things to consider before we decide to retire, and we'll take a look at them in the next chapter.

Summary

- Investing is a good and wise use of the money that God gives us to steward on his behalf, but we must be ever vigilant for the temptations of pride and greed.

- Understanding the risk/reward dynamic is essential, as is knowing your risk tolerance.

- There are a wide variety of investment types and styles, but most professionals agree that diversification is critical. And your ability to control your emotions and not buy or sell at the wrong times is more important to your long-term success than the specific investments you choose.

- Once you decide on a long-term investing strategy, stick to it; consistency, especially in the face of economic cycles and market ups and downs, will pay off in the long run.

- Costs matter. There are many low-cost (and even no-cost) investment options available, so it makes little sense to pay high fees, even for the best-performing investments, as they can add up over time.

For Reflection

- Do you understand the difference between a trader and an investor? Which are you? Which do you think is most appropriate for long-term retirement planning?

- Has God shown you any areas of greed or pride when it comes to your motivation for, or attitude toward, investing? What can you do to change?

- How confident are you in your investing knowledge and skill? What can you do to better educate yourself?

- Do you have an investment strategy that you think you can stick to through thick and thin?

Chapter 7

DECIDING TO RETIRE

"You are never too old to set another goal or to dream a new dream." —C. S. Lewis

"For which of you, wanting to build a tower, doesn't first sit down and calculate the cost to see if he has enough to complete it?" —Jesus Christ

In the first three chapters, we looked at retirement from several different perspectives and concluded that, for the Christian, retirement is permissible in Scripture since it isn't explicitly prohibited, providing it is done in a way that is consistent with biblical principles and values. Based on the assumption that most of us will retire someday, we discussed planning, saving, and investing for retirement in chapters 4, 5, and 6. So, we are anticipating a time when we will retire—either because we may have to or because we choose to do something different, for pay or not.

Not too long ago, if you were born a farmer, you died a farmer. If someone trained as a blacksmith, they hammered out horseshoes as long as they could. *How things have changed.* Now, if you want to start a new career at age 50, 60, or even older, you may be able to do so. And if you desire to work without having to be paid for it, you may think about retirement, which is a significant decision with huge spiritual, emotional, psychological, physical, and financial dimensions. In this chapter, we'll look at how you might go about making one of the most significant decisions of your life—the decision to retire.

Should You Retire?

You are getting close to 65, you've been working at your current job for more than 30 years, and your finances are in pretty good shape, so you're thinking about retirement. You'd like to spend more time volunteering at your church, in the community, and with your family, perhaps mixed with a little more travel and time for hobbies. *Should* you retire? It's easy to get excited about retirement and to dream about how you will spend your time. You may be looking forward to the flexibility and freedom that retirement can provide.

Others, understandably, have some reservations. They are concerned that retirement will be disorienting and boring, or they are worried about the lack of engagement with coworkers and others and the day-to-day challenges and opportunities their work provides.

The *should* question is one that only you can answer, and it's not a simple yes or no answer—there are many factors to consider.

Important Considerations

It would be good to have a clear direction and some plans in place for how you are going to spend your time in retirement before you retire instead of trying to figure it all out afterward. You will also need to understand your overall financial situation and whether you are able to retire (more on that later). Here are some basic questions that you may want to answer before you decide to retire.

What is God's will for you and your family?

When it comes to a major life decision like retirement, you need to know God's will. You can't just assume that because you may want to do something, it's what God wants you to do. God is pretty quiet in the Bible when it comes to the subject of retirement, so there are no hard-and-fast rules to follow. You are free to retire if you're able, to keep working another five or ten years if you want to, or even until you die (which is not very likely; most of us will have to retire sometime). But you need to seek God's will in this (Rom. 12:2). It's a very personal decision that requires careful consideration. It can also have a big impact on others in your life, especially family members, so they should be involved in the conversation.

Do you really want to leave your job?

Financial considerations aside, do you *want* to call it quits? A lot of people can't wait to hang it up, but others enjoy working and the benefits that come from it, both tangible and intangible. If your job is overly burdensome, tedious, or monotonous—one that literally saps the life out of you—you may understandably be anxious to retire. Perhaps you can use retirement as a time of greater freedom and flexibility but not one utterly devoid of any kind of work. God has designed us such that we make different contributions in various stages of life, and with age comes greater wisdom and experience, which helps us to contribute in meaningful ways (Job 12:12).

> A lot of people can't wait to hang it up, but others enjoy working and the benefits that come from it, both tangible and intangible.

Can you afford to retire?

This is one of the most critical questions you need to answer. It's so important that we'll go more in-depth with it later in this chapter. At the very least, it involves pulling together some essential information and doing some basic calculations to determine if you are financially able to retire. You will need to know what your expenses will be, your various sources of income, how much savings are required, and how you will convert your savings into a regular paycheck. (We'll discuss that at length in chapter 8.) More complex calculations are needed to if your situation is complex, or you want to determine how well positioned you are to deal with sequence risk, longevity risk, and inflation.

What will you do about health care?

If you are thinking about retiring before you become Medicare-eligible at age 65, you could be in a quandary about health care. Some will receive retiree health benefits through their employers (but that's mostly government employees); otherwise, you'll be on your own. You could sign up for COBRA for 18 months through your employer and then convert to an individual policy, but that means much higher costs. Other options include the Affordable Care Act (Obamacare), other private insurance, or a cost-sharing plan such as Medi-Share. These can also be very expensive, so for most, the best solution before Medicare eligibility is simply to keep working and stay on an employer-sponsored group health plan until at least age 65. (We'll discuss health care in greater depth in chapter 9.)

What will you do in retirement?

This is probably the question your spouse most wants you to answer. You will probably retire sometime in your 60s (the average retirement age in the United States is 63). If you are still reasonably healthy and active, you will be able to continue to both experience and contribute to the world and the people around you instead of aiming for a full-time lifestyle of leisure and recreation. You may have experienced a lot of joy and satisfaction from your job or career, but in retirement, you can go in another direction. The big question, then, is which way you will go.

Try to have some of that figured out before you retire. As it turns out, there are a lot of options to consider. Having the right answers to these questions can make for a smoother transition to retirement.

Can You Retire?

In theory, anyone could retire at any time. I've read about 20- or 30-something entrepreneurs who hit it big and retired. Others may have received a large inheritance or other windfall large enough to support their financial needs for the rest of their life. The emphasis here is on support their needs for the *rest of their life.* These people can afford to retire, or at least they think they can, and age and other factors may not have played much of a part in their decisions. But for most people like you and me, answering the "Can I retire?" question is more difficult.

CASE STUDY (PART 7): MIKE AND DEBBIE

Mike is now 57, and Debbie is 55, so they are in the all-important ten years or so before retirement. When last we checked in on them, they were in their early 40s, with three kids and a house, and Debbie was making plans to transition to a full-time mom. She made that change but had some health problems in her early 50s. Mike had to take a pay cut during a recession (thankfully, he didn't lose his job), but he's back above where he was before, making $82,000/year. They have continued to save regularly in

Mike's 401(k) and Roth IRA, but because of their portfolio's fairly aggressive risk profile (80% stocks), their investments took a 22 percent hit during that same recession. They were tempted to sell all their stock funds (the bond funds held their own) but didn't, and now the funds have recovered nicely, albeit after several very volatile years.

They have very little debt other than their mortgage, which now has a balance of $62,000 on the original $142,000 30-year loan. Their house's market value also took a hit during the recession, but it has recovered very nearly to its prerecession level, and is now worth more than when they bought it. Mike and Debbie would like to be mortgage-free before retirement.

All of their children are almost grown, and college expenses have taken a toll on their savings—they also took out a $20,000 second mortgage to help with that, bringing their total mortgage balance to $82,000. Fortunately, their house is now worth over $200,000, so they have built up a fair amount of equity, which may come in handy in the future.

Mike and Debbie currently have $528,000 saved for retirement. Looking again at Table 4 back in chapter 5, with an annual income of $82,000, they should be at about $574,000, so they are close. Mike and Debbie have started thinking about retirement. They will each be eligible for Social Security at age 62, but their full retirement ages are 66 and 10 months and 67, respectively. They are wondering if they might be able to retire early, perhaps by age 65 (when they are Medicare-eligible), to transition to some kind of full-time ministry or mission work (and not necessarily for pay). That may be feasible if they get their first and second mortgages paid off and continue to keep their monthly expenses in check.

There are some key milestones that affect everyone when it comes to retirement. First, you can't usually withdraw money from defined contribution plans such as 401(k)s/403(b)s, or IRAs, without paying taxes and penalties until age 59½. Next, there is the earliest age that you can start receiving Social Security benefits, which is 62, but your benefits will be permanently reduced if you do. Company and government pension funds typically have similar restrictions and start payouts from age 62 and beyond. Another critical milestone is age 65, when most people become eligible to receive Medicare health-care benefits. Finally, there is your full retirement age, as defined by the Social Security Administration, which for most baby boomers is age 66, but if you wait until age 70 to start receiving benefits, they will be substantially (32%) higher. If you have reached these milestones, you are in what financial planners call the retirement red zone.

To truly answer the "Can I retire?" question, we have to do the seemingly impossible, which is to make certain projections based on many unpredictable variables. We don't know how long we will live; nor do we know what our actual expenses will be due to inflation, health issues, or other variables. We also don't precisely know what our income will be (some of it will be fixed, and some will be variable based on our investments and savings withdrawal strategy). If there is any good news here, it's that even though these are unpredictable and therefore unknowable to us, God knows and controls all things (Ps. 147:5; Col. 1:17; Jer. 32:27). Consequently, we need not be overcome by doubts and fears about the

> Consequently, we need not be overcome by doubts and fears about the future; ultimately, our hope and trust is in the God who has said, "My plan will take place, and I will do all my will" (Isa. 46:10b).

future; ultimately, our hope and trust is in the God who has said, "My plan will take place, and I will do all my will" (Isa. 46:10b).

In spite of the economic uncertainties, answering the question "Can I retire yet?" from a financial perspective is a relatively simple calculation, which can be done manually or with the help of a retirement calculator.[1] It involves determining whether you can cover your estimated monthly expenses in retirement with your monthly income—the same thing you have to do before you retire—but with income from different sources, such as Social Security, pensions, annuities, and savings. The following approach, graphically depicted in Figure 9, is one you can use on your own, but you may be better off working through this process with a fee-only financial planner/advisor; this is especially true if your situation is more complicated than what I cover here. The basics will mostly be the same, but your financial professional will incorporate the unique factors and nuances of your retirement scenario.

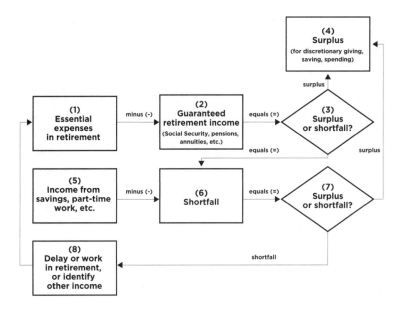

FIGURE 9: "Can You Retire?" Decision Diagram

Decision Process Overview

First, we have to get a handle on what our expenses will be in retirement, differentiating between *essential* versus *nonessential* expenses. Second, we need to identify and quantify all *guaranteed* income sources, which include pensions, annuities, and Social Security. Third, we want to know if our guaranteed income will cover our essential living expenses. If so, we are technically able to retire, but we may be on a very tight budget. If they don't cover it, we have a shortfall and need to determine if it can be covered by income from savings, which is the last piece in the puzzle. If that handles it, but just barely, we will remain on a tight budget. If we have something left over, we will have room for some discretionary giving and spending.

1. Estimate your essential living expenses

The number that we need to begin with is your *estimated essential living expenses*—what you think your bills will be in retirement. At a minimum, you need to cover your truly *essential* living expenses (food, clothing, shelter, transportation, taxes, medical expenses, tithe, etc.). You will need to decide what that list looks like for you, but to start out, try to include just those things that are *nondiscretionary*. That will provide you with the expense baseline that you need to be able to fund. And remember, although you need shelter, you don't necessarily need a five-thousand-square-foot house with a large mortgage. Some retirees choose to live in a "tiny house" or an RV. Your essential expenses need to be reasonable in proportion to the amount of income you will have to cover them. They are the bare minimums that you need to fund in retirement. If you can support more than that, then all the better— you'll have some discretionary funds to work with.

If you have a budget and have already been tracking your expenses, this should be reasonably straightforward. You could use your current numbers, but you may want to make some adjustments for living in retirement. Some costs will stay the same; for example, your utility bills if you remain in your home. Others may go up or down due to a change in location or lifestyle. There will probably be some employment-related costs that will go down. These include Social Security and Medicare tax withholding since they will go to zero when you stop receiving a paycheck. Your contributions to retirement accounts may stop, and you may no longer pay certain union fees and professional costs. If you commuted to work, those costs might be eliminated, but you may be going to other places. Your payments for employer-sponsored disability and life insurance costs may go away unless you convert to private insurance. Other miscellaneous expenses, such as clothing and other personal items and eating out, may be less as well.

If you haven't been tracking your expenses, you could calculate them starting with a set of basic expense categories and then by going through your financial account statements to come up with an estimate for each category. Adjust the categories that you think will change after you quit working. If you want to make a quick, high-level assessment, you could use a percentage of your preretirement income (usually between 60% and 100%). Regardless of which approach you choose, don't forget to plan for unpredictable expenses. The best way to deal with these expenses is to establish a contingencies fund and to assume that you will need to replenish it from time to time and include that in your essentials budget. If you don't, you will end up having to take it from other savings, or worse, put it on a credit card.

2. Calculate your guaranteed income

Once you have a handle on your *essential* expenses, the next step is to determine how much you will have from *guaranteed* income sources. This includes income from Social Security, government and company pensions, and annuities.

Social Security: The best way to get this number is to go to the Social Security website and use their Retirement Estimator.[2] You can use the tool to get an estimate of your benefits based on different retirement date scenarios. Keep in mind that the earlier you start receiving benefits, the lower they will be. Another important consideration is that both you and your spouse may be eligible to receive Social Security benefits even if only one of you has been employed. Under current rules, non-employed spouses or those who have not earned sufficient work credits on their own are eligible to receive 50 percent of the qualifying spouse's benefit. This is a great help to many couples, especially those who will rely mainly on Social Security for income in retirement.

Pension: Most companies have done away with defined benefit (pension) plans or are in the process of doing so. The main exceptions are local, state, and federal governments. If you are one of the fortunate ones who will receive pension income in retirement, you just need to get an estimate of your benefits from a plan statement, your employer's pension website, or by contacting your human resources department. Similar to Social Security, pension plans may pay different amounts depending on when you start receiving benefits and the survivor benefit option you choose. You may also have different payout options, such as full or partial lump sum, monthly, quarterly, or annual payments. Most people will select a monthly payment option with a spousal survival benefit.

Annuity: If you purchased an annuity before retirement, you could elect to start receiving regular annuity payments any time after you retire (or after age 59½ if it is in an IRA). The size of the payout will depend on the amount of principal that is annuitized (converted to a stream of regular payments), which is based on the annuity purchase amount plus any growth (if it is some kind of deferred income annuity) and your age when you start receiving payments. Depending on the terms of your annuity contract with the insurance company, those payments are guaranteed for life.

3. Determine if you have a surplus or shortfall

As Figure 9 shows, this involves some simple math to determine whether you will have sufficient *guaranteed* income to cover your *essential* living expenses in retirement. You need only to subtract your total essential expenses from your total guaranteed income to see whether you have a surplus or shortfall. Most people will find that they have the latter, but you may be an exception if you have a substantial Social Security benefit in addition to pensions and/or annuities. A surplus means that your guaranteed income exceeds your estimated essential living expenses, which can be considered discretionary income. If you have a shortfall, then you will need additional income to meet your essential expenses and possibly provide for some discretionary spending as well. This is where your retirement savings come in.

4. Add income from savings

In addition to your guaranteed income sources, you will also want to know how much income you need have from your retirement savings—your 401(k), 403(b), IRA, and similar accounts to help cover your essential expenses. The challenge with these accounts is that income of any amount is not guaranteed and can vary greatly based on financial market dynamics and your individual withdrawal strategy. Unless your money is in federally insured investments,[3] such as certificates of deposit (CDs), these accounts can go down, thereby making distribution amounts uncertain.[4]

If you are very close to retirement, coming up with a total should be reasonably easy. You just need to look at your most recent statements and add them up. Next, you would calculate the amount that would have to be withdrawn from your savings to cover any income shortage. An example of this calculation is illustrated in Table 10. As shown, you have a preretirement income of $75,000, essential income in retirement of $58,500, Social Security of $42,750 (guaranteed), which resulted in a shortage of $15,750 per year. Once you come up with a savings total ($450,000 in this case), you can now express the annual shortfall as a percentage simply by dividing the total amount of your assets by the amount of your annual shortfall—in this example, $15,750 divided by $450,000, which equals 3.5 percent. So, your required savings withdrawal rate needed to cover the shortfall is 3.5 percent.

Income before retirement:	$75,000
Estimated income required after retirement:	$58,500
Less Social Security	($42,750)
Equals surplus or (shortage)	($15,750)
Total retirement savings	$450,000
Savings withdrawal rate ($15,750 / $450,000)	3.5%

TABLE 10: Savings Withdrawal Rate Calculation

Another way to do this is to multiply the savings amount of $450,000 by the so-called "safe" withdrawal rate of 4 percent (.04), which is $18,000/year. In our example, that would more than cover the $15,750 shortfall with a surplus of $2,250. In either case, you would be in pretty good shape since, as we shall see in the next chapter, a required withdrawal rate of 3.5 to 4.0 percent is generally considered to be *sustainable* over a long retirement. Obviously, the greater the shortfall in your guaranteed income relative to your essential expenses, the higher your required withdrawal rate from savings will need to be to cover it. Similarly, the lower your total retirement savings balance, the higher the withdrawal percentage may need to be. If your required withdrawal rate is too high (higher than 5 percent), sustainability will decrease dramatically, increasing the likelihood that you will run out of savings sooner than you would like.

5. Decide if you still have a shortfall

If you have gotten this far and have found that you have an income shortfall, or that your required withdrawal rate is relatively—perhaps even prohibitively—high, you may be tempted to become anxious or fearful. That isn't the goal of this exercise, but it's better to understand the realities of your situation than not. You can continue to work and save and invest, or you could look for other sources of income, such as converting some of your savings to an immediate annuity, tapping into home equity, working part-time, or starting a small business in retirement. If your retirement equation doesn't produce the numbers you'd hoped, remember that your heavenly Father knows your situation and will give you the understanding, wisdom, and knowledge you need to do the best you can with whatever God has given you to steward— before and during retirement (Matt. 6:34).

If the Answer Is "No"

If, for whatever reasons, you decide that you just aren't ready to retire or that you aren't able to, you have some options:

Keep working in your current job

If you have concluded that you aren't financially ready to retire, at least not yet, and if you are not working in a position that makes you miserable and is ruining your health, then you could just continue to work beyond your originally planned retirement date. You can use that time, even if it's only a couple of years, to delay Social Security to increase benefits and also to save more.

Try to improve your situation at your current employer

For those who just don't like their job, or are finding their work increasingly difficult, perhaps there's something you can do about it. Try to find ways to improve your situation at your current job. Maybe you can get a different job, work schedule, or even a new boss at the same company. If you are bored and unchallenged, let it be known that you want a more meaningful assignment. In other words, don't just go with the status quo if there's anything you can do about it, especially if you may need to stay for a few more years.

Change employers

Another possibility is to continue to work full-time but not for your current employer. You may have concluded that you can't influence the things you don't like, so positive change is unlikely. If you do decide to make a change, this could be a more challenging option than the others. Even though it can be difficult to change jobs when you are older, many employers are beginning to recognize the value that mature, experienced, knowledgeable, and responsible workers can bring. Those with highly transferrable skills may have an easier time, all the more so if the skills are highly specialized and in demand. You may also be giving up some very lucrative financial benefits such as stock options, pension vesting, and other things like extra vacation time, so give this decision careful thought.

Work part-time

Many people work part-time as they transition to full retirement. Some have referred to this as "pretirement." This could mean working less in your current job or taking a part-time job doing something entirely different. The goal of this approach is to continue to work while freeing up time to do other things. But working less means less income, which is fine if you can supplement it with some of the other income sources we have already looked at. However, if you are behind in saving for retirement, it may be best to continue to work full-time. Either way, working and delaying Social Security for a few more years may be just what you need to do to ensure that you have enough income down the road.

Do something totally new

Finally, you could retire and work at something entirely new. This could be a second, or third, career or business that you've dreamed about having someday. If you decide (or have to) retire on somewhat shaky financial ground, then finding meaningful work for pay will be a necessity. Plus, you get the additional benefits of working at something you love. You may not have the same energy, stamina, or effectiveness you did in your earlier career, but that doesn't mean you can't find the right thing in retirement.

Finding the perfect work isn't easy no matter what stage of life we're in. If you feel stuck in your current situation but are unable or simply don't want to retire, then put together a plan to get yourself unstuck. To help you, I have included some resources in the appendix. There are opportunities out there, but you may need to create your own, which may be especially appropriate for those with an entrepreneurial bent. On the other hand, if you want to retire and have sufficient resources to do so, then you have the freedom to retire and spend your time in service to God and others.

Summary

- Before you decide to retire, there are at least two crucial questions that you need to answer: "Should I retire?" and "Can I retire?" The first has mostly to do with physical, emotional, and spiritual components; the second is mainly financial. Both need to be addressed as they are critical parts of the retirement decision process.

- Should you determine that you can't retire, you have options. These include working longer in your current job, working to improve the situation in your current position, changing employers, shifting to part-time work, or doing something entirely new.

- It is much better to work a little longer than to retire too soon, only to find out that you are unable to make ends meet later on. If you want to retire and can afford to do so, then use it as a time to ramp-up your activities in support of your family, church, and community.

For Reflection

- Have you considered all of the critical questions that need to be answered before you decide to retire? Which is going to be the most difficult for you?

- Do you want to retire but are discouraged that it doesn't appear feasible at this time? Based on what you read in this chapter, do other options come to mind? What do you need to do to make retirement a reality?

Part Three

REIMAGINE YOUR LIFE IN RETIREMENT

Chapter 8

FUNDING YOUR RETIREMENT

"Even if your investments are going down, don't worry. You have quality investments with long track records. They will come back—just like they did the last time you considered bailing. Besides, you don't need your whole nest egg at once. You just need some of the income from it." —Dave Ramsey

"When you don't know what the answer is, you know *Who* the answer is." —Larry Burkett

As we discussed in the chapter on investing, a helpful perspective on retirement planning is to view it in two major phases: the *accumulation* phase and the *distribution* phase. For most people, the accumulation phase begins in their 20s or 30s (sometimes later) and continues into their 60s or 70s. A great thing about investing during this time is the ability to weather market ups and downs. Even if we haven't saved enough or there are big market drops just before you retire, you may have the option of postponing retirement until you are in a better position. But once we enter the distribution phase, we don't have that option, as we will no longer be adding to our savings and have to start living off them instead.

This is when things can get dicey. If we retire at age 68 and live to age 88, we will be in the distribution phase for 20 years! Estimated lifespans are increasing, so some will live even longer, which puts an increased burden on us to manage our spending and assets wisely during retirement to try to ensure that we don't run out of money before we run out of life. Our goal in retirement is to be a non-borrower and not be become an unnecessary financial burden on our families, our churches, or the government (1 Thess. 2:9).

Living in retirement now is very different than it was 30 or 40 years ago. Back then, a lot of folks had defined benefit pensions, which, along with Social Security, provided them with a solid income floor for retirement that was virtually guaranteed. They received monthly income just like a regular paycheck. But today the majority of retirees have to rely on Social Security and savings only to fund their retirement. (Remember our shaky three-legged stool from chapter 1?) They have been used to getting a regular paycheck for 30, 40, or maybe 50 years and may occasionally dip into savings to help with ordinary or extraordinary expenses, but most are reluctant to do so. Retirement changes that paradigm completely as a significant amount of income must come from savings unless their expenses are very low and Social Security benefits are high. This is the challenge we will discuss in this chapter: how to generate income in retirement that will last as long as we do.

The Challenge: Income for Life

As if the usual risks to our investments such as volatile markets and inflation aren't enough, the risk that our savings and the income they provide won't last as long as we do is one of the greatest. Retirement planning professionals call this longevity risk. I know it may seem strange to call it a *risk*, since a long life is generally considered a blessing

(Deut. 5:33). But in this context, it is a genuine risk that has to be reckoned with.

According to figures from the Society of Actuaries, a 65-year-old man has a 41 percent chance of living to age 85 and a 20 percent chance of living to age 90. A 65-year-old female has a 53 percent chance of living to age 85 and a 20 percent chance of living to age 90. The percentages are even higher for couples. If the man and woman are married, they increase the likelihood that at least one of them will live longer. There's a 72 percent chance that one of them will live to age 85 and a 45 percent chance that one will live to age 90. There's even an 18 percent chance that one of them will live to age 95.[1]

Income planning is one of the most challenging (and often debated) areas of retirement planning. Financial advisors are, for the most part, more focused on the accumulation phase than the distribution phase. Most, if they are reasonably competent, can guide a future retiree through the accumulation phase reasonably well. They are adept at things like asset selection and allocation, dollar-cost averaging, dealing with tax issues, and steering clients through inevitable market ups and downs. In fact, some of this is increasingly being put on auto-pilot due to new financial technology such as "robo advisors," which use artificial intelligence to optimize retirement portfolios. But income distribution planning is more difficult, and there is much more at stake. A market crash or two during the accumulation phase may not wipe out someone's savings, but if a retiree mismanages their savings and income from age 65 and beyond, the negative consequences can be significant.

Income Floor with an Upside

A widely accepted approach to creating sustainable lifetime income is known as creating an income floor with an upside. This builds on the guaranteed and flexible income sources we discussed in chapter 7. This strategy, which is sometimes described as "safety first," is becoming increasingly popular with professional retirement planners/advisors.

The essence of it is that a retiree devotes some amount of assets to creating a lifetime stream of guaranteed income with the rest dedicated to an investment portfolio for liquidity and the possibility of future growth.[2] Figure 10 depicts the income floor with an upside approach, which will be the basic framework we will use in this chapter to develop an income plan in retirement. The upside, which is made possible by market-based investment assets such as stocks, also has a downside, as it isn't guaranteed and, in a worst-case-scenario, could be completely depleted prematurely due to high withdrawal rates, extremely poor returns, or both.

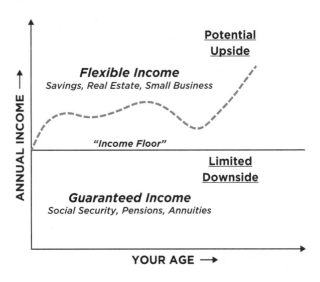

FIGURE 10: Income Floor with an Upside

Optimally, we would be able to meet all of our retirement spending needs (essential expenses and something for discretionary spending as well) with guaranteed income from things like Social Security, pensions, and annuities—your income floor. However, most will find that they need some amount of flexible income to supplement things like Social Security and a pension to fund their retirement.

As shown in the next diagram, Figure 11, the income floor is created using various types of guaranteed income. (Most retirees will have Social Security, at a minimum.) The income upside comes from flexible income sources that have the potential to provide additional and possibly increasing income as we progress through retirement. (The most common is income from retirement savings.)

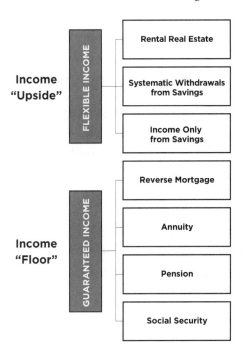

FIGURE 11: Retirement Income Types

Some retirees will be able to meet 100 percent of their income needs in retirement using only guaranteed income, but most will probably use some combination of the two plus a cash bucket for emergencies. Part-time work, starting a business and other kinds of self-employment can also be used, but are outside the scope of what we will look at in this chapter.

Establishing Your Income Floor

Once you decide to retire, you have to put an income plan in place, and that starts with creating and optimizing your income floor. Each guaranteed income source presents its own set of options and choices, so making the right decisions is very important.

Social Security

Social Security will be an integral part of most retirement plans, making up anywhere from 25 percent of income for wealthier retirees with income over $100,000/year to 75 percent or more for middle-income and lower retirees with incomes of $50,000/year or less. Generally speaking, your claiming strategy is how you optimize Social Security income in conjunction with the income you will have from other sources. The more limited your income is from other sources, including savings, the more critical it is to optimize your Social Security benefit. A strategy of delaying benefits until at least your full retirement age (FRA) or to age 70 (but no longer), if possible, is the best way of maximizing the contribution that Social Security makes to your guaranteed income floor.

> **Key Concept:** *Social Security* is NOT an account with your name on it that you draw from in retirement like a 401(k) or IRA. It functions more like a lifetime, inflation-adjusted annuity that is paid out of an insurance trust that is administered by the Federal Government.

The amount of your Social Security benefits is mainly determined by how many years you worked, your earnings record while employed, and the age you claim your benefits. Deciding when to claim Social Security benefits is one of the most critical retirement planning decisions you will make. Currently, over 60 percent of retirees take benefits at age 62. Claiming benefits is soon as you're eligible at age 62 will permanently reduce your monthly payments by 25 percent. If Social Security will be approximately 50 percent of your retirement income, then your total income is reduced by 12.5 percent (25% of 50%) for the rest of your life. If you were born between 1943 and 1954, and wait until age 66, you will receive 100 percent of your full retirement age (FRA) benefit. And if you can wait until age 70, your benefits increase significantly to 132 percent of your FRA benefit, which is an increase of 8 percent a year! (The FRA gradually increases to age 67 for those born in 1960 and later. They will realize a 124 percent increase by delaying until age 70.)

The rules on Social Security are more complicated than you might think, especially if you are a couple trying to optimize your joint benefit claiming strategy. The decisions you make will affect both of you while you are living as well as the future income of the surviving spouse (usually the wife). One of the main aspects is the spousal benefit, which is the greater of the spouse's earnings on their own record or one-half of the primary recipient's benefit. Every couple's situation is different, so I would strongly urge you to research this using the resources in the appendix and also to meet with a Social Security counselor if necessary.

Defined Benefit Plan (Pension)

If you have a pension, you may find that it will not provide you with all of the income you need in retirement. But for some, it will be a substantial portion and, when combined with Social Security, may provide you with all you need. As we alluded to in chapter 7, you may have different distribution options: lump sum versus lifetime payments, and so forth. If you choose a lump sum distribution option, then you can't include that in your guaranteed income stream going forward. That's because you will have to do a lump-sum roll-over into a qualified retirement savings account such as an Individual Retirement Arrangement (IRA). This is a very, very important decision that should not be taken lightly so make sure to do your homework before you decide to do it. If you take a lump sum, you will have to figure out a way to construct your own private pension to create an income stream from those savings, which is what this chapter is all about. For that reason, many people would do better to take the lifetime distribution instead. Plus, your employer pension payments may be higher than what you could get with a personal annuity or other options.

Annuities

Like Social Security and pensions, annuities are considered low risk. Although annuities can produce guaranteed income, that doesn't mean there are no risks. In a worst-case scenario, there is solvency risk, but even that is mitigated to some extent by federal guarantees. Some may have deferred annuities that were purchased before retirement. But the more likely scenario is that, after you retire, you may decide to use some percentage of your retirement assets to purchase a lifetime income annuity (also known as a Single Premium Immediate Annuity, or SPIA), or one of its more complex cousins, a variable or fixed index annuity. Using some of your savings to purchase an annuity to help create a guaranteed income floor in retirement is becoming an increasingly popular approach, especially when you combine an annuity with Social Security to produce enough income to meet all your essential living expenses for as long as you live. The difficulty is getting comfortable with the idea of handing over a big chunk of your savings to an insurance company and then figuring out what kind of annuity and how much to purchase.

Do you need an annuity? Generally, the lower the percentage of your *essential* living expense that Social Security and perhaps a pension cover, the greater the benefit of an annuity to help secure your income floor. If your flexible income sources are large, you may be less inclined, or you may purchase a smaller annuity contract. Also, the more conservative your risk profile, the more likely you may be to purchase an annuity.

How much of an annuity do you need? Everyone's situation is different, but consider purchasing the smallest annuity that meets your needs, and if possible, keep it at around 50 percent or less of your retirement savings. (Many retirement professionals suggest 25 percent to 30 percent.) You want to use the savings that remain to be invested more aggressively with the opportunity for future growth and discretionary income. This strategy is consistent with the income floor with an upside approach we have been discussing—the annuity adds to the income floor and the funds you retain can help provide the potential upside. You can find more resources about annuities in the financial resources section in the appendix of this book.

What kind of annuity should you purchase? There are two basic categories of annuities: *lifetime income annuities* and *variable and fixed-index annuities*.[3] The first are contracts with an insurance company where you give them a single lump sum, and the insurance company then pays you, and perhaps your spouse, a fixed amount every month for as long as you live or for a certain number of years—called period certain. Generally, the older you are when you purchase the annuity, the higher the payout will be. The biggest differences between this type of annuity and the variable and fixed-index kind are that the latter tend to be costlier and more complex. That may or may not be a show-stopper for you, as they offer add-on benefits that are not available with the lifetime income variety.

To be fair, variable and fixed-index annuities may have some upside potential that is not available with lifetime income annuities. Variable annuities use underlying investment subaccounts, which are similar to mutual funds, and can, therefore, take advantage of possible market growth. They also offer various types of guarantees, such as a guaranteed minimum withdrawal benefit, which guarantees a certain level of income regardless of market performance. Some also offer a guaranteed death benefit, which ensures that you or your family would get back no less than what you invested if the market crashes. (Note that these all come at a cost in the form of contract riders.) Fixed-index annuities offer principal and interest guarantees, and your principal doesn't go up and down as it does with a variable annuity. Instead, the guaranteed interest accrues based on the performance of a market index, such as the S&P 500.

Deciding which of these annuities is best for your situation can be a difficult task. You will probably need to consult with a trusted financial/insurance professional, but keep in mind that many are paid by commission, which could create a conflict of interest; try to find a fee-based advisor instead. More conservative retirees may lean toward the lifetime income annuities, whereas more aggressive investors (who have more confidence in the financial markets) may gravitate toward a variable or fixed-index annuity to capture better returns, but they will need to be comfortable with higher risk, market volatility, and cost.

Reverse Mortgage

Retirees who have a lot of home equity but limited income resources in retirement may be good candidates for a reverse mortgage. They can be used as another source of guaranteed income, much like a pension or annuity.

These instruments have traditionally gotten a pretty bad rap—and for a good reason. High up-front costs and interest rates along with tight lending restrictions gave them a pretty negative reputation. But improved federal rules and regulations and lender practices have made them a more available and suitable option for many. Nowadays, you can take advantage of a federally insured Home Equity Conversion Mortgage (HECM) if you are age 62 or older and need to turn home equity into a guaranteed income stream in retirement.

> **Key Concept:** A *reverse mortgage* is what it sounds like: a mortgage loan that provides regular payments to the borrower. The loan doesn't have to be repaid until the owner dies, moves, or sells the home. The loan balance grows as payments are disbursed, including interest.

Like annuities, reverse mortgages can be difficult to understand, especially the "small print" in the mortgage contracts themselves. Therefore, it's essential to do your homework and make sure you know exactly what you are signing. When you sign up for one, you aren't giving up the title to your home, and you can live in it as long as you maintain it and pay the taxes and insurance (you can even use the mortgage proceeds for that purpose). You will also never have to repay the loan unless you choose to. However, once you move or pass away, the house will have to be sold or refinanced by your heirs to satisfy the mortgage debt, which includes accrued interest. This results in a smaller estate that can be passed to heirs. They aren't for everybody, especially those who don't plan to live in their homes for very long. But if you have a few options, this is certainly one to consider to help build your guaranteed income floor.

Treasury Inflation-Protected Securities (TIPS)

TIPS are a unique type of investment that I have chosen to include as another option for building your guaranteed income floor. In fact, some retirees may limit their investments in stocks, bonds, CDs, and the like and instead decide to invest the majority of their assets in TIPs. That's because TIPS are bonds issued by the US Treasury that pay interest *and* are guaranteed to be adjusted for inflation. The real yields of TIPS, which is the interest rate paid after inflation, tends to be low, typically in the 1 percent to 3 percent range,[4] but the US Treasury adjusts the yield to account for inflation. For example, if inflation is 2.5 percent, a TIPS bond paying 1 percent would actually pay 3.5 percent until the bond matures. For that reason, and because they are backed by full faith and credit of the US government, they are one of the safest investments available. You can purchase TIPS directly from the US Treasury online when they are auctioned, or you can buy them in mutual funds or ETFs in a brokerage account.[5]

Options for Generating Flexible Income

Having an income upside may be more critical during the early years of retirement when we, hopefully, have greater health and energy and are therefore more active and inclined to spend more on activities and travel. As we enter the middle years, we may still be in good health but less motivated to travel or spend on other activities. Then there are the later years when physical and/or mental limitations or other health issues will probably slow us down even more. We may actually spend less during this time despite increased medical and perhaps long-term care expenses. But, "real" spending may increase due to the effects of inflation.[6]

There are several other potential sources of income in addition to the guaranteed ones we have discussed so far. These are the various ways of tapping into the retirement savings you may have in 401(k)/403(b)/457(b) and IRA-type accounts.

Withdrawal Rules

Before we discuss some specific flexible income strategies, we first need to briefly consider the IRS rules regarding withdrawals from retirement savings accounts. These include the "Rule of 55," the "Early Withdrawal Rule," and the "Normal Distribution Rule." (We will discuss the Required Minimum Distribution Rule later in this chapter.)[7]

As a general rule, any withdrawals from a 401(k)/403(b)-type account before age 59½ (the Normal Distribution Rule) result in a 10 percent penalty plus the payment of ordinary income tax. There are some exceptions, however, which include disability, certain legal rulings associated with a divorce, and leaving a job after age 55—which is the "Rule of 55"—in which case you can make early withdrawals, but only from the assets that are in the retirement savings plan that is maintained by your former employer.

Early withdrawals from traditional (non-Roth) IRAs also get hit with the same 10 percent penalty plus taxes. IRAs have most of the same exceptions to the penalties as a 401(k) does—death, disability, divorce, and so forth. One twist with IRAs is that you can withdraw money early if you use it for a qualified education expense (like college), medical expense (above 10% of your gross income), or a first home purchase.

But just because you can withdraw certain funds without a penalty doesn't mean you should. Assets that you withdraw between age 55 and 59½, or beginning at age 59½, will no longer be working for you earning dividends, interest, or capital gains over the long term.

Withdrawals from Roth accounts are treated differently because they are not tax-deferred, they are tax-free. That means that distributions taken after age 59½ are tax-free provided you have held the Roth IRA for at least five years. Like other retirement accounts, there is a 10 percent penalty for early distributions, but it is only applied to earnings, not the original amounts invested; you can always withdraw your original investments tax- and penalty-free before age 59½. This is just one of the reasons why Roth accounts are such powerful and flexible savings tools.

Income from Savings (Capital Preservation Strategy)

This strategy assumes an income-only portfolio orientation, which is very popular with many retirees. It further assumes that the passive income from your investment portfolio, when combined with your guaranteed income sources, is at least equal to what you need to spend on living expenses. Finally, it also assumes that your investments will grow more than the average inflation rate (total return minus income). This typically requires some kind of conservatively allocated stock/bond portfolio that generates stock dividends and interest income, but it could also come from real estate or even a small business. And unlike a total return approach, which we'll look at next, it is focused on maximizing income from the dividends and interest with less of a focus on capital growth. The assets that generate this income are rarely sold to raise cash, so the overall value of the portfolio would not go down except in cases of poor market performance.

This approach has several benefits. First, you don't have to sell assets early in retirement that could be used to generate income in the future. Second, if the markets perform poorly during those early years but continue to generate sufficient income for your needs, you can avoid locking in investment losses early in your retirement. (This helps mitigate the sequence of returns risk we have discussed previously.) Of course, should your interest and dividend income be significantly reduced, you may be forced to sell some assets to generate income.

The challenge with this strategy is that conservative income portfolios don't typically generate 4 percent or more of income in low-interest-rate environments, nor is any of it guaranteed (like TIPS). So, you may have to take more investment risk to meet target income requirements, and greater risk means that it's more likely that your assets could lose value. If you do have to dip into your principal for additional income, one way to do that is to sell assets that have done well over the last year. This is really just a way of rebalancing your portfolio to reestablish your targeted stock/bond percentage mix (50/50, 60/40, 40/60, and so on).

Systematic Withdrawals (Total Return Strategy)

This option assumes that you have a diversified portfolio of stocks and bonds that is focused on total return. This approach can be used during both the accumulation and distribution phases, typically with a shift toward a more conservative asset allocation during retirement.

Key Concept: *Total return* describes a way of investing that seeks to maximize the performance of an investment or a pool of investments through growth (capital gains), interest, dividends, and distributions over time. In other words, it's not focused on either growth or income exclusively but seeks to achieve both.

Fixed withdrawals use a total return approach to investing and can be easily implemented with just a handful of low-cost mutual funds or ETFs that cover the growth, value, and income spectrums. You can achieve this strategy by choosing either actively managed or passively managed funds, and then simply make regular withdrawals from interest and dividends, and also by selling appreciated assets as necessary, perhaps through rebalancing.[8]

There are two variations to the fixed withdrawals strategy—fixed *amount* and fixed *percentage*. With a fixed amount, you calculate how much money you need from savings to add to other sources of income and withdraw the same amount each year (monthly, quarterly, or annually), regardless of what the markets do to the value of your investments (you may adjust this withdrawal for inflation). With this approach, you will have a predictable income, but the negative is significant. Because you are not accounting for changes to the value of your investments, you could run out of money much sooner than expected.

The most common strategy is the fixed withdrawal method. Using this approach, you would withdraw the same percentage from your savings each year, perhaps adjusting for inflation. Because it is a percentage, the amount being withdrawn may vary as the value of your investments fluctuates. This is often referred to as the 4 percent rule that we discussed earlier. Withdrawing much more plus decreases for inflation increases the risk of portfolio depletion later in life; withdrawing less decreases the risk.[9]

Flexible withdrawals are based on variable market performance data and take into account how the financial markets—and therefore your investments—perform from year to year. This approach is a little more complicated than fixed withdrawal, but it can be more effective in the long run. Like the fixed withdrawal strategies, it assumes a total return-based approach to portfolio management.

If they can, most people will reduce their spending during declining market years, which we could describe as adaptive withdrawals. If you prefer a more formulaic approach, consider a variable withdrawal strategy consisting of a fixed percentage with some boundaries—stability with flexibility. One such approach is called the 95 percent rule. With this approach, you withdraw 4 percent of your portfolio *or* 95 percent of whatever you withdrew the year before, whichever is greater. That means you would not reduce your income by more than 5 percent in any given year, even if your assets lose more than that. This provides some stability and adjustments based on market performance; however, in a prolonged market downturn, it would have a substantial cumulative adverse effect on your income, and your spending would need to be reduced accordingly.

There are other options for flexible withdrawals which are more complicated and vary your withdrawals in direct proportion to market performance. They look at historical market performance metrics and help you decide if stocks or bonds are valued more highly at a given point in time. These include a last year performance strategy, which only looks at which performed best in the previous year, and also the 3-year and 7-year moving average strategies, which look back for those periods to determine the best performing asset class. Current year withdrawals are then made accordingly. If average stock returns are higher than bonds, withdraw from stocks. Conversely, if bonds returns were greater than stocks, withdraw from them instead.

Yet another strategy uses something called "CAPE" (stands for Robert Shiller's Cyclically Adjusted Price-to-Earnings ratio), which is the price of the S&P 500 divided by the average of the last ten years of earnings and adjusted for inflation.[10] If the CAPE is higher than its long-term median, then we can assume that stocks are highly valued and withdraw entirely from them. If it is below its median, then we would withdraw from bonds.

The Bucket Strategy

This is a variation of the total return approach, and has become a popular approach for managing income distributions in retirement. It is also known as a time segmentation strategy because it breaks retirement down into time lines which correspond to buckets and allocates assets to them based on volatility and when you'll need the money. As shown in Figure 12, most bucket strategies have at least three buckets: short-term (1 to 3 years), medium-term (3 to 7 years), and long-term (7 years and beyond). The assets in each bucket become increasingly risky as time frames elongate. For example, bucket one may hold only cash and equivalents, bucket two would be filled with short- and intermediate-term bonds and dividend-paying stocks, and bucket three might contain high-yield bonds and growth stocks. You may see this as a typical balanced asset allocation portfolio; in many respects it is. If you hold 10 percent cash, 30 percent bonds, and 60 percent stocks, then you have a basic 60/40 portfolio.

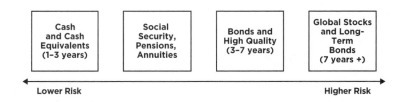

FIGURE 12: The Bucket Strategy

The anchor of this strategy is the cash bucket (years 1–3), which gives you a spending buffer in addition to Social Security, pensions, or annuities, and helps to avoid sequence risk. In other words, it buys you time to ride out a down market. Meanwhile, the income bucket (years 3–7) is generating income while controlling risk with the use of fairly stable bond and high-quality stock funds. The idea is to use the income from bucket two to refill bucket one. Bucket three (7+ years) remains untouched, and over time the riskier investments hopefully go up in value. They can then be sold to refill bucket two.

This is a pretty good strategy; most people with a balanced total-return-oriented portfolio will use something similar since the question eventually comes down to whether and when you have to sell riskier equity assets to generate income.

CASE STUDY (PART 8):
MIKE AND DEBBIE:

Mike and Debbie are now 65 and 63 respectively, and Mike would like to retire so that they can start a nonprofit ministry to the homeless in their city. They have been planning accordingly—their house, including the second mortgage, is paid off and they have no other debt. They have been diligent in continuing to save 15 percent for retirement, and their savings balance is now at $864,500. (Although their asset allocation has become more conservative—they are now at 60 percent stocks and 40 percent bonds, they have averaged 4 percent a year over the last nine years.) Their prospects for retirement to start a full-time ministry seem promising, but let's see if they can pull it off.

Living expenses: Mike's and Debbie's current income is $88,000, and they think they can live on 80 percent of that (or $70,800) in retirement. That equates to $5,900 per month.

Estimated fixed income: Their estimated Social Security income would be approximately $3,000 per month ($2,000 for Mike and $1,000 for Debbie, which is 50 percent of Mike's based on the spousal benefit). They have no additional fixed income from pensions or annuities.

Estimated flexible income: Applying the basic "4 percent rule" to their savings of $864,000, they can withdraw $34,560 per year or $2,880 per month (their "safe" withdrawal rate).

Total income: When combined with their Social Security, they will have an income of approximately $70,560, which is just under their target replacement amount of $70,800.

This quick and simple analysis would seem to suggest that Mike and Debbie would be able to retire as planned. The key will be for them to keep their living expenses in check so that they can live on 80 percent or less of their pre-retirement income.

But what if their situation was different—a lot different?

Assuming that their Social Security benefits remain unchanged, but their savings are 50 percent less (or $432,000), what do their retirement prospects look like? If they stick to a 4 percent withdrawal rate, their flexible income will drop to $1,440 per month, reducing their total income to $4,440 per month, which is $53,280 per year (a shortfall of $17,520). Perhaps they can live on that. If not, what are their options?

First, they could simply delay retirement. This would be the least desirable option, as Mike and Debbie want to start their ministry to the homeless as soon as possible. Another option is that one of them could continue to work for pay to make up as much of the $17,520 as possible, but they would prefer not to do that either. Annuitizing some of their savings might help, but the impact would be relatively modest. That leaves tapping into their home equity. There are basically two ways to do that:

Downsize. Mike and Debbie could downsize to a smaller house (or perhaps a very low-cost rental). For example, if they can sell the house for $240,000 and buy a small condo for $120,000, they could invest the difference of $120,000 and generate $400 per month in additional income. But that would still leave an annual income deficit of $12,720.

Take out a reverse mortgage. A second option is to take out a reverse mortgage, which could provide Mike and Debbie with annual income in the $6,000 to $12,000 range. At the high end, it would make retirement a little more feasible, but reverse mortgages come at a price: high fees, high interest rates, and loss of home equity that could have been used later in retirement as a cash reserve. If they are comfortable with that, they would still have to figure out how to live on approximately $5,000 less income per year. This is a sacrifice they may be willing to make to pursue their calling to start their ministry.

Understanding Required Minimum Distributions (RMDs)

This is sometimes overlooked until it's too late. Tax-advantaged accounts such as 401(k)s, 403(b)s, 457(b)s, and IRAs that were set up as deductible accounts (meaning you made pre-tax contributions) will typically be taxed when withdrawing from them in retirement. To make sure it eventually gets its due, the Federal Government has rules called Required Minimum Distributions, which go into effect on April 1st of the year you turn 70½. The rules stipulate the minimum percentage you must withdraw each year and include in your taxable income. They apply to the account owner and also surviving spouses. (Non-spousal beneficiaries or heirs must follow the Stretch IRA rules, which we will look at in chapter 10.) Currently, the percentage starts at 3.65 percent and then increases each year after that. By the time you turn 90, you'll have to withdraw 8.77 percent, and more if you live even longer.[11] If you fail to withdraw the required amount, you'll be hit with a tax penalty of 50 percent of what you should have withdrawn.

RMDs can be used as a framework for regular withdrawals from your flexible income sources. If you wait until age 70½, you would start with the minimum (currently 3.65%) and increase it each year based on the RMD minimums. If you start earlier, consider withdrawing 3.5 percent each year until you reach age 70½ when you have to follow the IRS rules.[12] Your RMD will quickly reach 4 percent (at age 73) and then go higher from there. The actual amount you have to withdraw each year will be determined by a combination of your age, the size of your portfolio, the rate of return for the portfolio of IRA assets, and the IRS-mandated withdrawal rate. Because of the increasing required withdrawal rate, there is a high probability that RMDs over a longer than average lifetime will substantially deplete the residual value of an IRA. However, although the money must be withdrawn and the taxes paid, it does not have to be spent; it can be reinvested in a taxable non-retirement brokerage account and used when needed in the future.[13]

The RMD rules are relatively straightforward, but as with other things like rollovers and Roth conversions, it may be a good idea to discuss this with a financial advisor, especially if you are close to age 70½.

Decide on a Withdrawal Strategy but Stay Flexible

The plan you employ will depend on your spending needs and available income sources in retirement. Ideally, your income will be a little higher than your expenses. Using the income floor with an upside approach means that you will optimize your guaranteed income sources to cover as much of your essential expenses as possible. If it doesn't satisfy them completely, then you will need to tap into flexible income sources if you have them. Once you decide on a plan, remain flexible. It may be necessary to adjust spending, or your withdrawal rate, or both. (It's also possible that you will want to go back to work for a while if you are able.) A flexible withdrawal rate tied to market performance probably offers the best chance for success.

> **Once you decide on a plan, remain flexible. It may be necessary to adjust.**

The bottom line is that it would be folly to enter retirement without a good idea of how you're going to convert your savings into a sustainable stream of income to last the rest of your life.

What if Your Income Isn't Enough?

If you've done your homework and concluded that you don't have the income you will need, you have some options. One possible solution, though not necessarily the most popular one, is to delay retirement and keep working and saving. The longer you save and delay Social Security, the higher your retirement income should be. You can also decide to spend less, perhaps much less than you did before you retired. Another option is to work part-time in retirement—the extra income can make a big difference. Finally, you can accept a lower probability that your savings will last. But be careful, this can be risky. If you decide to take additional risk and withdraw 5–6 percent versus the 3–4 percent that is typically recommended, the probability that you will outlive your money will increase significantly, at least statistically speaking.

Once you've decided on an income strategy, you are ready to look at other important things like housing, health care, insurance, taxes, and giving in retirement. We'll discuss these next in chapter 9.

Summary

- Choosing and implementing a strategy for lifetime income is one of the most significant challenges in retirement, perhaps more so than accumulating assets during the saving phase. It is also of the utmost importance, as running out of money before you run out of life is a highly undesirable outcome.

- A helpful way to think about this problem is to create an income floor with an upside using guaranteed and flexible income sources. The goal is to cover as much of your essential expenses as possible with guaranteed income and use flexible income for discretionary expenses.

- Most people will benefit from the assistance of a fee-only financial planner/advisor in constructing an income plan for retirement that minimizes the risk that they will run out of money before they run out of life.

- Annuities have traditionally had a bad rap, but recent research suggests that they should be a part of most retirees' income strategy. As with all financial products, there are good ones and bad ones. If you decide to purchase, use a broker/ advisor without a potential conflict of interest (paid on commission).

- There are multiple options for calculating your withdrawal rate, the most common being the so-called safe withdrawal rate. This approach is increasingly being called into question as being dated and no longer appropriate for present-day realities. Therefore, consider the alternatives and use the one that makes the most sense for you.

- If you come up short, consider delaying retirement so that you work longer, save more, and delay Social Security to maximize benefits.

For Reflection

- Have you given more thought to the accumulation phase than the distribution phase? What do you think God is leading you to do to wisely plan for that important time?

- Are you anxious or fearful about your ability to come up with a satisfactory income plan in retirement? What do you know about God and his character that can help alleviate your fears?

Chapter 9

LIVING IN RETIREMENT

"Faithful servants never retire. You can retire from your career, but you will never retire from serving God." —Rick Warren

"Taxes, after all, are the dues we pay for the privileges of membership in an organized society." —Franklin D. Roosevelt

In previous chapters, we looked at some of the "big pillars" of retirement planning: saving, investing, and income distribution strategies. But there are numerous other things to be thinking about and planning for that have to do with the practical aspects of living in retirement—things like housing, work, health care, insurance, taxes, and other financial concerns, which we will delve into in this chapter.

Where to Live

Many people entering retirement consider relocating for a variety of reasons. Others decide to "age in place" in order take advantage of familiar surroundings and perhaps to stay close to family and friends. Many move into retirement communities that have sprung up all over the country, especially in the warmer regions of the country. What you decide to do will probably be based on several important considerations.

Expenses Matter

Retirees who live in a high-cost-of-living area may want to move somewhere less expensive. There can be a big difference, for example, between some areas of the Northeast and Mid-Atlantic and the Southeast. The West Coast is notoriously expensive, especially as compared to the Midwest and Southwest. So, by relocating, you may be able to significantly reduce housing expenses, including taxes, insurance, and utilities, and also groceries, gas, and certain services. Retirees need to make housing decisions that work for their anticipated income level, since it is typically the most significant expense they have to deal with in retirement.[1] If you don't get that right, everything else can be negatively impacted.

Optimally, you will enter retirement with a paid-for house that costs a reasonable amount to maintain. Carrying mortgage payments into retirement can create a burden, and although it's certainly possible to retire with a mortgage, you will need a large sum in savings just to make the payments. To illustrate, suppose you have a principal and interest mortgage payment of $1,000 per month, or $12,000 per year. Based on a 4 percent "safe" withdrawal rate, you would need savings of $300,000 ($12,000/.04) just to handle the mortgage.

If your housing expenses are disproportionally high, you may have some options. You could downsize into a smaller residence, perhaps in the area where you currently live. Depending on how much equity you have, you may be to reduce or completely eliminate your mortgage payments. Another option is to sell your home and rent something with a lower monthly cost; you could use the proceeds from the sale to generate extra income toward the rental expense. A third option is to refinance your mortgage to get a lower monthly payment. In any case, you want to avoid early depletion of your savings due to high housing costs. You also want to prevent a forced sale of a primary residence due to an inability to pay the mortgage in retirement (or, in the worst-case scenario, loss via foreclosure). Finally, you don't want to lose the ability to use housing equity for funding retirement expenses in the future, such as for long-term care, should you need it.

Climate Matters to Some

In addition to the overall cost of living, some retirees also consider the weather. Larger homes cost more to air condition in the summer and heat in the winter, and downsizing may help with that. Plus, those living in colder northern climates tend to gravitate toward the warmer southwest or southeast. I grew up in Florida and many who moved there are shocked by just how hot and humid it is most of the year, especially if they had visited only during the cooler winter months. We live in North Carolina now, which has a more temperate climate, and I understand we have a lot of "half-backers" here—retirees from the north who find places like Florida or Arizona too hot and move halfway back to more moderate regions.

Relationships Are Important

A lot of retirees move to be closer to family, especially grandchildren. My wife and I have grandchildren ourselves, and live near most of them. It is great to be able to see them from time to time and to be a part of their lives. But this is one to be careful about, since some young families will move several times and you could get stuck somewhere after your family has moved on. In addition to our families, we have other relationships—our church, social network, service providers, and so forth. These things may lead you to consider staying put. As part of a local church, you are needed right where you are, as others need the unique contribution that only you can make based on the gifts that God has given you (Rom. 12:4–8). Because of this, you should always at least consider your church before deciding to make a move.

What to Do in Retirement

As we saw in chapter 2, because we were created by God and in his image, work is an integral part of his great design for our lives. This doesn't change just because we are retired from a full-time, paid position. In retirement, we may no longer need to earn a living, but we can still do "good works"—things that contribute to the good of others and the furtherance of God's kingdom on the earth.

Created for Good Works

Paul, in Ephesians 2:10, says, "For we are His creation, created in Christ Jesus for good works, which God prepared ahead of time so that we should walk in them" (HCSB). The word *walk* in the Bible usually refers to a way of living, a lifestyle. So, what Paul is talking about here is a life of good works performed by God's grace, for his purposes, and for his glory.

God created us for many purposes, and one of them is to bring honor and glory to him by using our unique callings and gifting to serve God and others. In 1 Corinthians 10:31b, Paul instructs us to "do everything for the glory of God." Similarly, in Colossians 3:17, he urges us to do whatever we do "in the name of the Lord Jesus, giving thanks to God the Father through him." Therefore, as we grow older and wiser, we should view ourselves as God does—a masterful creation with the high honor and purpose of doing everything in the name of the Lord Jesus, by his grace, in his strength, under his authority, and for his eternal purposes. Work in this context is not necessarily about having a job (although it could be), but the variety of ways we can image our Creator and serve others in retirement.

What Kinds of Good Works?

So what are some of the good works God has prepared for us in our 60s, 70s, 80s, and beyond? As shown in Figure 13, it all begins with the gospel and all that it entails at the center of our lives; the main point is that all that we do, in whatever sphere we do it, is because of, and for the sake of, the gospel.

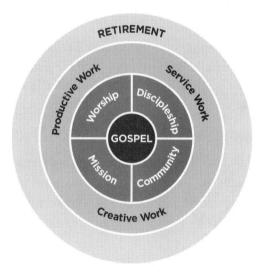

FIGURE 13: Good Works in Retirement

We can begin by listing the normal, everyday things Christians do as part of their spiritual lives: worship (attending services, praying, celebrating the ordinances, and sacrificial giving); discipleship (studying the Scriptures, growing in the fruit of the Spirit, practicing the spiritual disciplines, and hearing and obeying God's Word); community (participating in a small group, pursuing accountability and encouragement, using our spiritual gifts, serving others in need, and training and equipping others); and mission (evangelism, pursuing biblical justice and mercy, participating in or supporting church planting, and engaging and impacting society). These should continue, and perhaps intensify, as we age and for as long as we are able. They are the essentials that are fundamental to living gospel-centered lives, and as also shown in Figure 13, they can find expression in a variety of ways in different kinds of work that we may do in retirement.

The different types of good works we can do that are part of a God-glorifying retirement lifestyle can be described as creative work, productive work, and service work. While none of these are as important as our spiritual endeavors, they do flow from our spiritual endeavors, and are a part of God's plan for our lives.

Creative Work

We were made in God's image, with a desire to create, just as God created. Not in the same way that God did, of course, but as a natural expression of the creative gifts we have been given by our Creator-God (Gen. 1:27). Creativity is one of the many ways we can image our Creator.

You may undertake creative work for the sheer joy of it, and as a way to enrich the lives of others. Perhaps you'd like to leave something behind that inspires, entertains, or informs those who come after you. If you are gifted in photography, painting, writing, music, or a special craft or skill, retirement may give you more time for the kinds of creative expression you already enjoy. Even if you don't *feel* gifted, retirement may give you the time to experiment—to explore different things and discover the creative gifts God has given you to enjoy and bless those around you.

I like to play the guitar and write. My wife is the real "creative" in the family and is particularly gifted in arts and crafts.[2] We don't strive for perfection; in fact, we are far from it. We enjoy these things without concern for how well we perform, although we try to do the best we can. We do them because God has given us the ability to do so, because they bring us joy, and as a way to bless others.

But most important, our creative gifts reflect the small divine deposit of God's glory that he has put in each of us, and using them can be an act of worship that ultimately points back to him.

Productive Work

Others may pursue work that they view as more productive. That could mean a paid position, such as starting a second career or a small business, but there are many ways one can add or create value that benefits others, that may or may not involve making a profit. Just because you are no longer in a traditional job doesn't mean you can't do productive work. Rather than viewing retirement as a "way out" of a job you don't like, view it instead as a means to do something new, perhaps without the immediate financial pressure to earn a living.

Because retirees are living longer, healthier lives (60 is the new 40, right?), they have an opportunity to continue to pursue productive activities and interests well into their 70s or 80s. Consequently, older workers are starting businesses at a rapid rate. Half of small business owners are over 50. The majority (86%) of them did so by either founding or buying independent for-profit businesses; the rest purchased franchises.[3] And according to a 2016 study, 24 percent of new businesses are started by people between the age of 55 and 64.[4] These newly minted entrepreneurs cited an unexpected layoff and difficulty finding a new job as the predominant reasons.

"Staying in the game" as an independent contractor, consultant, or small business owner is an excellent way to create an income stream in retirement. It can allow you to delay Social Security benefits and to continue to add to your retirement savings if you need to. One note of caution: If you transition from employee to freelancer or small business owner, and your primary need entering retirement is income, you may need to have a cash reserve or other income to live on as the ramp-up time may take awhile. And you certainly don't want to take on a lot of debt. If you have something that is already going, and you think you can grow it quickly after you retire, that could be a great way to start with some inertia behind you.

Instead of starting a business from scratch, you could consider part-time or seasonal work. There are a lot of websites out there for retiree jobs: RetiredBrains.com, Encore.org, RetirementJobs.com, Workforce50.com, and Workamper.com, to name a few.

Service Work

Work that focuses on service to others in our families, churches, and communities can also be particularly joyful and satisfying in retirement. As Christians, we know that serving others is one of the things we are called to do—it is an integral part of what it means to be a disciple of Jesus. But how we do so will vary with our gifting and calling. Without the responsibility of a full-time job, retirement can provide greater freedom to pursue good works that utilize our God-given talents and abilities to serve God and others in the ways we are most passionate about.

When we were younger, we may have been too busy with a career and family to serve outside our homes or businesses as much as we would have liked. Retirement can be an opportunity to set out on a new path for serving others. As we continue to pursue the priorities of worship, discipleship, community, and mission, these can be demonstrated in different contexts. For example, volunteering at a local homeless shelter is service work, which is a part of mission and community, and having a heart for the homeless comes out of worship and discipleship (Matt. 25:35–40). Serving in children's ministry in your local church is a way to disciple others, and it is part of our mission to "make disciples of all nations, baptizing them in the name of the Father and of the Son and of the Holy Spirit, teaching them to obey everything I [Jesus] have commanded you" (Matt. 28:19–20), which includes the not-yet-believing children in our church community.

I have always enjoyed working with children (I have been teaching second graders in my church's children's ministry for many years), and after I retired in 2018, I started volunteering as a reading tutor in a local Title 1 elementary school.[5] It's a blast, and although the kids may feel like their grandpa is in the classroom, they don't seem to mind.

Others may want to get more actively involved in social or political causes. I know several older Christians who are very active in pro-life causes.

Another avenue for good works that can combine all three types (creative, productive, and service) is to start up a nonprofit. There are many causes that Christians are passionate about, and creating a nonprofit to advance them may be just the thing for you. Building a nonprofit from the ground up involves a lot of work and can be just as challenging as starting a small business, perhaps more so. But it is a wonderful way to serve others through the creative use of the skills and talents God has given you, and also to involve others who share your passion. A nonprofit can produce a product, provide a service, or take the form of a ministry—the possibilities are almost endless.

Natural aging will eventually slow us all down, but it need not mean the end of a life of active service to God and others. It can lead to a change in roles and responsibilities from that of an active worker to more of a teacher, mentor, and supporter. In fact, I think that is part of God's glorious plan and purpose for his people (2 Tim. 2:2; Titus 2:2–4; Heb. 13:7).

Health Matters

Maintaining our health as we age can be both challenging and costly. Yet our ability to retain our strength and vitality in retirement for as long as possible will help us to do the good works God calls us to do. Life will eventually take its toll, and although we do what we can to remain healthy and active, we know that ultimately "the course of [our] life is in [his] power" (Ps. 31:15).

Medicare Health Insurance

Medicare is a health insurance program run by the US government whereby it subsidizes medical insurance for certain disabled individuals and everyone who has reached 65 years of age. (This generally applies only to citizens and legal immigrants.) Almost all retirees will be eligible for Medicare health insurance when they turn 65. Even if they didn't work long enough to qualify, they can still receive certain benefits by paying for them. Early retirees (that is, before age 65) have to find an alternative, perhaps through the Affordable Care Act (ACA), private insurance, or a cost-sharing program such as Medi-Share, until they reach Medicare eligibility at age 65.

Medicare has four parts. They are identified as Part A, Part B, Part C, and Part D.[6] (Welcome to the alphabet soup world of Medicare!) Each part has specific deductibles and benefit limits.

Part A (hospital coverage) comes at no charge to you and your spouse if you have at least 40 Social Security wage credits. Part B (medical insurance) pays for doctor's bills. Part B is optional, and you are charged monthly for this coverage, but the government pays about 75 percent of the cost.

Things get a little more complicated with the other parts, because some combine what others cover (such as Part C, which is known as Medicare Advantage insurance and covers Parts B, C, and D).

Furthermore, some cover what others don't (such as Part D, which is for prescription drug coverage and includes some of the costs not covered by Parts A or B.)

In addition to the parts, Medicare Supplemental Insurance (known as Medigap Insurance) is also available and, depending on what plan you select, it can significantly reduce your deductibles and may increase the benefit maximums of Parts A and B.

Most retirees would do well to consider a Medigap policy. They are offered through private insurance companies, but the plans they offer are specified by the government. The retiree pays a monthly premium—the amount varies based on which plan is selected. Prescriptions can be a big part of retiree medical expenses, as some prescription costs are not covered by Parts A or B or Medigap plans, which is where Part D comes in. As with Medigap, many providers offer different coverages and costs, which can vary by geographic region and plan specifics. The good news is that the Federal Government pays about 75 percent of the standard coverage costs, and the states also pay some. Retirees who use a lot of prescriptions will want to consider this part. Dental and vision insurance coverage are also available as separate policies under Part D.

One of the most critical aspects of Medicare is the sign-up rules. If you don't sign up at the right times, you could be charged higher premiums. The sign up window for Part B is a seven-month period that begins three months before you turn 65 (3 months prior and 4 months afterward). After that, you will pay a 10 percent premium for each 12-month period of delay. The exception to this rule is if you are covered by an employer-provided health-care plan. Once you leave your employer, you have eight months to sign up and avoid the late enrollment penalty. You could also get hit with a Part D penalty if you go 63 or more days in a row without prescription drug coverage after you qualify for Medicare. And last but not least, there's a six-month window beginning the month you turn 65 when you have a guaranteed right to buy any Medigap policy, after which you could be charged higher premiums or denied coverage.

Planning for Health-care Expenses

Health-care costs will likely be one of your most substantial expenses in retirement. Although they may vary significantly from person to person, those who enter retirement with a chronic condition that requires regular medications, treatment, or doctor visits will have higher expenses than those who are basically healthy. According to a study by Fidelity Investments, a couple who retired in 2018 will need about $280,000 in some combination of savings and income to cover their health-care costs, including Medicare expenses but not out-of-pocket expenses or long-term care costs, which could take it much higher.[7] Therefore, it is imperative to plan for health-care expenses as part of your retirement budget.

Most retirees will rely on their savings and other income sources such as Social Security, pensions, and annuities to pay for health care in retirement. But a great way to save specifically for health care before retirement and reduce your taxable income at the same time is with a Health Savings Account (HSA). Think of them as a health-care IRA. You are eligible to contribute to an HSA if you are participating in a high-deductible health insurance plan as so defined by the IRA. The contribution limits in 2019 are $3,500 for an individual and $7,000 for a family. If you are age 55 or older, you can contribute an additional $1,000 per year. You can't contribute to an HSA after you enroll in Medicare, but you can withdraw the money tax-free to pay for medical expenses not covered by Medicare.

Do You Need Life Insurance?

The primary purpose of life insurance is to replace an income-earner's income in the event of their untimely death. It is wise to have life insurance when you are younger and you have a family that is depending on you for income. But do you need life insurance in retirement?

The simple answer is, "not necessarily, if you are already self-insured," meaning that you have sufficient resources in the form of Social Security survivor benefits, pensions, annuities, and savings to support your surviving spouse and any other family members who depend on you for support. You also don't need to buy one of those burial policies that are sold on late-night television programs. However, if you are living on a minimal fixed income (such as Social Security) with little or no savings or other income, a small, very low-cost policy may be beneficial to help with debts and final expenses. Alternately, you could save the premiums to build up a small cash reserve, which could be used for these purposes in the future.

What about Old Policies?

Many retirees may find that they have an old policy that they have had for many years. It may even be a whole life policy that has been completely "paid up" with dividends and regular payments. If that's you, discuss it with your agent. Payments made to a paid-up policy will probably increase both the cash value and the death benefit. For those who don't need that additional growth, it may make sense to reduce their premium payments or stop them altogether. Some people buy life insurance as an investment vehicle; keeping it for its tax advantages while also maintaining the death benefit may make a lot of sense.

If you have a fixed-term plan with ten years or longer remaining, you might want to keep it if you or your spouse, or someone in your immediate family, would be left in severe financial jeopardy should you die prematurely. This is especially true for those who need to earn some income in retirement. If kept in force, a term policy could be used to make a large gift at death or to cover taxes, debts, or other expenses. Additionally, if you are caring for someone with special needs whom you want to be sure is well taken care of long after you are gone, it may come in handy for that as you could use the proceeds to fund a Special Needs Trust.[8]

Consult your insurance professional before you cancel or "cash-in" any existing life insurance policies. Because life circumstances change, your agent may suggest replacing your policy with a better one. And while you're at it, review all policy ownership and beneficiary arrangements to ensure they are still consistent with your desires.

The Long-Term Care Conundrum

Many retirees will require some amount of long-term (nursing home) care during their lifetimes.[9] The costs are significant, are not covered by Medicare, and the odds that you will need it are fairly high. It certainly isn't going to bankrupt everyone who has to go into a nursing home, but it can take a big bite out of your savings.

The solution that the insurance industry has put forward is Long-Term Care Insurance (LTCI), which does exactly what it says: it insures you against the potentially *catastrophic* cost of extended care, meaning many years, not days or weeks or even a few months. LTCI can protect your savings from being depleted, which would result in you having to revert to Medicaid to pay for care.

Not surprisingly, LTCI is expensive and, depending on when you purchase it, you could be paying premiums for 20- or 30-plus years. Plus—and this is a real kicker—the premium is not "fixed"; the issuing company can increase it at any time in the future. Altogether, these things make LTCI policies themselves a little risky. Another difficulty with LTCI is that it may not insure you against a "worst-case scenario." They have limits, and most agents recommend policies that cover at most three to four years of care. LTCI can also be difficult to get due to the stringent underwriting requirements.

The financial analysis to make a rational decision about LTCI is difficult, mainly because we don't know what future LTCI premiums will be, how long we will be paying them, what the limits on benefits will be, or what our actual need for LTCI will be, if at all. Many LTCI policies are sold on the basis that it can protect your assets, but once you are retired, you will be using a significant part of your assets to pay the premiums, possibly for several decades. If you choose not to buy it, you may have to spend down your remaining retirement assets to effectively self-insure for whatever long-term care you need, and some people would rather not have to do that. A significant chunk of your assets will go toward paying for it, one way or another.

I can't tell you that you should or should not buy LTCI; I think it is a very personal decision. As with any insurance scenario, you need to weigh the costs against the probability of a particular occurrence (the risk). The most critical part of the whole equation seems not to be whether we will need long-term care at some point in our lives, but for how long and at what cost. If, as some studies have confirmed, long-term care is a high-probability but relatively low-cost occurrence due to short duration, then spending a ton of money on premiums may not make sense if you are in a position to self-insure or believe that you have family members who would be able to help care for you. As we saw in chapter 1, families have historically cared for each other and should always be the first option if available. Different types of care options are also emerging, such as in-home care. There are also all kinds of new medical technologies coming on the scene: remote sensors and alarms, health monitors, and assisting equipment. We may even have robots to help one day!

You may want to purchase LTCI for the peace of mind it offers, but it may not be the blanket of financial protection that it is often sold as. While it may not fully protect your savings, it will definitely defray some of the costs, especially in a worst-case scenario. If you do decide to purchase it, the younger you do it, the better because premiums will be lower. You will be paying them for a more extended period of time, and depending on how much they increase, you may not break even, which strengthens the case for self-insuring. If you believe that you can set aside some amount of savings, or perhaps a deferred income annuity, for future long-term care expenses, that may be a better option.

Taxes in Retirement

Christians are commanded to pay our taxes, and we should do so with gratitude and integrity (Rom. 13:6–7). And since death and taxes are both certainties in life, almost everyone will pay some taxes in retirement. The main exception is those living on Social Security alone who will pay little or nothing.

In 2019, the standard deduction for married-filing-jointly is $24,400. The tax rate for taxable incomes less than $19,400 is 10 percent; it's 12 percent for incomes from $19,400 to $78,950; and 22 percent for those with incomes of $78,950 to $168,400.[10] These rates are some of the lowest in decades, so retirees with gross incomes between $30,000 and $60,000 will pay very little. For example, a couple receiving $25,000 in Social Security and $25,000 from savings (total of $50,000), will have taxable income of $21,850. Their tax would be $2,234, which is an *effective rate* of only 4.8 percent.[11]

> **Key Concepts:** Your *effective tax rate* is simply your average tax rate. It is typically lower than your *marginal* tax rate, which is the rate at which your next dollar of income would be taxed.

Wealthy retirees will always have large tax bills—how large will depend on the laws and the marginal rates in effect at any given time. As of 2019, the current law is supposed to be in effect until December 2025, but things could quickly change with shifts in the political winds.

Your Types of Retirement Income Matter

Retirees who mainly rely on income from Social Security and little else probably won't pay any tax, since deductions will substantially reduce their taxable income to near zero. Those who have significant income from other sources, such as a pension, annuity, or taxable retirement savings account, may have to pay taxes on up to 85 percent of their Social Security benefits along with the taxes on the other income as well. How much tax will depend on their taxable income and their corresponding *marginal* tax rate.

Income withdrawals from retirement accounts such as 401(k)s, 403(b)s, 457s, and IRAs are typically taxable and have to be reported on your return where they will be added to your Social Security and any income from other sources, such as a pension or annuity, to come up with a total. An exception is when you withdraw from a Roth account; they are usually tax-free if done correctly. Pension and annuity income is typically taxable as well, especially if funded with pre-tax dollars. Lump-sum distributions from these types of accounts that are properly rolled over into an IRA aren't taxable until you start withdrawing from them. Your final tax liability is determined on your taxable income (adjusted gross income minus any credits and deductions) and your effective tax rate for that year.

You will need to plan for taxes a little differently in retirement since they won't necessarily be withheld like they were when you were receiving a regular paycheck. That means you may have to take care of your own withholding to make sure you comply with IRS rules. Although the IRS doesn't say that you *must* have taxes withheld from retirement account distributions, they can hit you with a penalty if you owe more than a certain amount (currently $1,000) and haven't either 1) made quarterly estimated tax payments, or 2) had sufficient funds withheld from the distributions.[12] The second approach is preferred by most retirees, and a good default withholding rate is 10 percent, since that is a pretty accurate measure of what a typical taxpayer will owe on their IRA distributions. If you anticipate having a lot of income, you may want to go a little higher.

Other Financial Matters

There are some additional financial considerations that relate to maximizing tax savings in certain scenarios involving retirement accounts.

IRA Rollovers

In your earning years, the majority of your retirement savings will be in employer retirement accounts—401(k)s, 403(b)s, and the like, and perhaps a pension plan. However, when you leave one job for another or leave the workforce altogether, you may want to consider taking advantage of an IRS provision known as a roll over.[13]

This provision is most often used when the funds in a 401(k) or 403(b) type account are rolled over (directly transferred) into a

Traditional IRA or Roth IRA. This is usually advisable due to the lower cost and wider set of investment choices that will be available in the IRA. It can also be used to roll over a lump-sum distribution from a defined benefit (pension) plan, although you should seriously consider taking it as a lifetime annuity instead. But that would only make sense if you could get a better payout from the insurance company than your pension fund. No matter what, be very careful to execute the roll over correctly, or you could end up paying taxes or even penalties; it's best to have the financial institutions involved handle it directly for you as what is known as a trustee-to-trustee transfer.

Roth Conversions

Many retirees have not considered a Roth conversion. It is something that may make more sense before you are in retirement, but at the very least it is worth learning about and possibly discussing with your financial advisor. The primary purpose is to convert taxable IRA assets to nontaxable assets in a way that is consistent with IRS rules.

Key Concept: A *Roth Conversion* is something else that the IRS allows whereby you can magically change a Traditional IRA to a Roth IRA *if* you meet certain conditions, not the least of which is having to pay all the taxes due on the converted amount in the year the conversion is executed.

Once you convert, you have to wait five years before you can start withdrawing from it. Before 2010, only people who earned less than $100,000/year could do a Roth Conversion, but that has changed; now people at all income levels can. Once you convert, your account has all the benefits of a Roth IRA. That said, the decision to do a Roth conversion is by no means a no-brainer because of the taxes you have to pay up-front at conversion to save on taxes in the long term.

None of us can predict the future, so we don't know what our tax bracket will be in 10 or 20 years. Taxes are a big factor in retirement planning and this uncertainty makes planning difficult at best. If you think your tax rate will be lower in retirement, hanging on to your Traditional IRA looks better—pay no tax now and low taxes in retirement. If you believe your tax rate will be higher, then converting to a Roth may be best in the long run—pay some taxes now at a low rate and none in the future when rates are higher.

Even if rates do go up, your income in retirement could be lower, so the impact may be negligible. Because 2019 tax rates are relatively low and the government's debt and spending needs are so high, higher rates are a likely scenario in the future. And since everyone's situation is different, and due to the complexities involved, I highly suggest you consult with a financial advisor before making a Roth conversion decision.

> **We will one day "retire from retirement," which is the day when we will leave this life and enter eternity.**

Many of you who are reading this will spend many years, perhaps multiple decades, in retirement. Wise planning and then living in retirement following biblical values and principles can result in a joyful and fulfilling life lived to the glory of God. But as we all know, we will one day "retire from retirement," which is the day when we will leave this life and enter eternity. This brings us to the final chapter, "Living and Leaving a Legacy."

Summary

- Once you make the decision to retire and develop a strategy to fund it, you will have other important choices to make. These include, but are not limited to, where to live and how you will spend your time.

- Health care is a significant concern for all retirees. Medicare will be the medical insurance that most retirees use, but with its various parts and providers, the choices can be overwhelming, so give yourself plenty of time to learn about it and then enroll in the plans that make the most sense for you.

- Retirees will spend a disproportionately high percentage of their income on health care, including Medicare premiums, so budget for it accordingly. Healthcare Savings Accounts (HSAs) are a great way to save money before retirement for medical expenses you incur later on.

- Most retirees will not need life insurance, but if you have an old policy, don't be too quick to abandon it.

- Long-term-care insurance is something that should be seriously considered by all retirees. However, it is costly and can be challenging to get if you have preexisting medical conditions. Plus, it may not protect you from a worst-case long-term-care scenario.

- Some retirees will pay higher taxes than others. Most retirement income will be taxable, but the actual tax you pay will depend on your taxable income and effective tax rate. Consult with a tax professional before making important decisions like lump-sum distributions from pensions and IRA roll overs or conversions.

For Reflection

- Have you thought about living in retirement as mainly a time for rest, relaxation, and fun, or as a time with greater opportunities to do the good works that God has prepared for you to do?

- If you are close to retirement, have you started to learn all you can about Social Security and Medicare, as well as other things like long-term-care insurance and taxes in retirement? If not, what can you do to start?

Chapter 10

LIVING AND LEAVING A LEGACY

"Beginning well is a momentary thing; finishing well is a lifelong thing." —Ravi Zacharias

"It ought to be the business of every day to prepare for our last day." —Matthew Henry

According to *Webster's Dictionary*, a *legacy* is "anything handed down from the past, as from an ancestor or predecessor." In his book *The Legacy Journey*, Dave Ramsey says that Christians should both *live* and *leave* a legacy. This idea of both living *and* leaving a legacy seems to capture the broad biblical perspective of the term.

For many people, when the topic of legacy comes up, they think "inheritance." There certainly is a financial and material component to legacy planning, but Ron Blue also reminds us that, "it encompasses the intangibles as well—wisdom, character, reputation, and memories."[1] Therefore, legacy and estate planning aren't just about leaving a large sum of money; they are about living a life that impacts others for their good and the glory of God (1 Pet. 2:12), not so that we will be remembered in a particular way, but so that we live a life "worthy of the calling [we] have received" (Eph. 4:1), and thereby bring honor and glory to God.

Living Your Legacy

Ask yourself this question: What will your family and friends say about you—or more important, the grace of God as evidenced in and demonstrated through your life—after you're gone? What will your God-glorifying life legacy be? These questions can help us to seriously consider how we should live our lives and steward all God has given us on this side of eternity. Stewardship isn't just about being debt-free or saving and investing to make sure we have enough to live on in retirement, important as those things are. It also includes what we do with the time, talent, and treasure God has entrusted to us and how we used them to contribute to the building of God's kingdom and the good of those around us.

> What will your family and friends say about you—or more important, the grace of God as evidenced in and demonstrated through your life—after you're gone?

Our legacy is not just about the money and possessions we may leave behind for others. It is the sum total of all the various ways we have been used by God while we were on this earth to impact the lives of others for their good and his glory. Therefore it's not just about leaving, but *living* a legacy—a life characterized by humility, kindness, integrity, trustworthiness, faithfulness, and generosity.

Many want to leave a legacy of wealth to their family and perhaps also their church and other ministries. But if what we leave behind is a financial legacy and little else, we will not pass along the godly wisdom, character, and life example to help ensure that the next generation wisely manages all God has given them for his glory.

The apostle Paul reminds us in 2 Corinthians 9:10–11 that what we sow and multiply in this life will "increase the harvest of [our] righteousness," so that we can "be enriched in every way for all generosity, which produces thanksgiving to God through us," even after we're gone. A legacy of lifelong generosity is one of the most God-imaging and glorifying things we can leave behind.

This can become more challenging in retirement when we probably won't be working for pay, and instead will be receiving income from other sources such as Social Security, pensions, and savings. Plus, our income may be less than when we were employed. A fear of not having enough may cause us to hold on to resources more tightly and not to be as generous as we have been. Our goal should be to continue to give consistently in retirement and budget it accordingly, regardless of the source of the income, and just treat it all as God's gracious provision, trusting God to "make every grace overflow to you, so that in every way, always having everything you need, you may excel in every good work" (2 Cor. 9:8).

Leaving a Legacy

I'm sorry if it sounds a little morbid, but retirement will end in your death.

This is the reality—each of us has an appointed time, and it isn't on any of our calendars, only God's (Heb. 9:27). That's one of the big challenges with this topic and how to plan—we don't know when (or how) it will come, just that it will.

Thinking about the end of our lives may be one of our least favorite things, but since we know it is inevitable, it is something we need to plan for. And remember, if you are a Christian, through the "Lord Jesus Christ himself and God our Father," you have been given "eternal encouragement and good hope by grace," which we can anticipate with great joy (2 Thess. 2:16). Although we look forward to heaven, one of the essential things we can do now is plan our legacy and how we want our resources to be used for the glory of God after we leave this earth.

There is something to be said for leaving a financial legacy to our children and others (money and possessions and how to steward them well). An oft-quoted Bible verse seems to support this: "A good man leaves an inheritance to his grandchildren, but the sinner's wealth is stored up for the righteous" (Prov. 13:22). Citing this verse, Dave Ramsey wrote: "Clearly the Bible teaches us to leave an inheritance for future generations . . . there's a biblical model for passing wealth generationally."[2] I would generally agree with Ramsey—there is a biblical model, but not *necessarily* a mandate. There is undoubtedly a command to provide for the basic needs of our family (1 Tim. 5:8), most important, our spouses. Leaving something to bless other family members beyond meeting basic needs, such as money for education or to pay off student loans, or to get rid of a mortgage, is indeed permissible, and generally good. But Ramsey also affirms that our legacy includes "an inheritance of character and of wonderful memories."[3] Hopefully, our legacy will be much greater than the material things we leave behind—a life of faithfulness, generosity, goodness, kindness, and compassion.

Our decisions about leaving wealth are very individual and personal ones. Some will exhaust all of their savings in retirement, so this won't even be a consideration. If you have resources left over and choose to leave everything to a church or a ministry of some kind or give it to the poor, you are free to do so. In fact, there may be times when it would be unwise to leave it to a family member if they don't have the desire or character to manage it wisely. Remember, it is still God's money, and as Ron Blue reminds us, our heirs may be poorly trained to handle an inheritance and, "Wouldn't it be a shame for your wealth to ruin your children or grandchildren? 'An inheritance gained prematurely will not be blessed ultimately' (Prov. 20:21)."[4]

It Begins with Planning

Leaving a legacy is possible through wise estate planning. Your estate is a great way to be a blessing to others after you're gone—your family, friends, and those in need—with a part of your lifetime increase in money and property. Lots of people think that only wealthy people with large estates need to be concerned about estate planning, but that is a wrong assumption. Everyone who will leave anything of value behind when they pass away should give this some thought.

There is a long list of things to think about before you finalize and formalize a written estate plan. Start by itemizing your priorities and commitments. Such a list may include children and grandchildren, but it could include other family members as well. It will most certainly take care of your spouse if you have one. Beyond your family, you may also feel a strong commitment to organizations like churches, charities, missions, and schools. If your estate is large, consider annual gifting before you pass away. You can do this using the Uniform Gift to Minors Act and can give up to $13,000 a year (married couples can give up to $26,000) without triggering any gift tax. This may reduce your final taxable estate, but you will experience the joy of giving while you are still alive.

Other considerations when coming up with an estate plan include things like the age (and competency) of children, special situations (such as a disabled relative), special handling of property, and so forth. These aren't necessarily complex legal questions, but they can be difficult and sensitive decisions due to their personal nature. There's no easy path for this unless you have no family or no assets, so it's best to just work through them one at a time. And remember, you can always make adjustments down the road if necessary.

Consider Using a Trust

Our stewardship obligations do not end after we are gone. Although we won't be there, we have a responsibility to ensure that the money that God has entrusted to us will be used wisely by those we leave it with. The younger that person is, the more likely that a large inheritance will be used unwisely. Estate planners suggest that a large inheritance may be better handled if it is distributed over a longer time, and perhaps at a later time when the child is older. Therefore, consider transferring a large inheritance over a period of years rather than all at once as a lump sum, especially if the inheritor is young, but also if older and lacking in character or in good money management skills. (Of course, you may want to reconsider leaving it to such a person in the first place.) A well-planned distribution strategy may include some principal up front, only income from the principal for a period of years, and then a final payment of deferred principal later on. Such an arrangement would require establishing some kind of *trust*.

> **Key Concept:** A *trust* is a legal fiduciary arrangement that allows a third party (the trustee), to hold and manage assets on behalf of a beneficiary or beneficiaries, which can include how those assets are passed to heirs.

Trusts are typically formed as part of your will but require a separate set of documents. They may or may not be fully funded at the time they are created, although some assets, such as real estate and financial accounts, may be transferred into the trust at that time. Additional funds, including life insurance proceeds, for example, can be added any time thereafter by the grantors of the trust. Larger and more complex estates, with many beneficiaries with conditions and timing such as what was described above, best lend themselves to be handled via a trust. If you have an unusually large estate and consult with an attorney, their tool of choice to avoid probate will often be a trust. However, if your estate is relatively small and non-complex, and your children are grown and on their own, you may have less of a need for one. Check to see if beneficiary designations and Transfer on Death/Payable on Death can do the job for you instead.

An excellent way to avoid putting your entire estate through probate is to create a revocable living trust. This type of trust is created while you are living, but you have to transfer your assets to the trust, which is typically accomplished by putting them in the name of the trust. It requires a lot of up-front time and effort, but doing it while you are alive is easier than leaving it for your executor to do after you are gone. The good thing about a trust is that it also enables you to specify the distribution of assets sometime in the future, perhaps conditionally, such as when children or grandchildren are headed to college, get married, or purchase their first house.

To provide for a family member who is physically or mentally disabled, you might want to consider a Special Needs Trust. This is a special trust for those who can't take care of themselves due to their unique circumstances. If the person qualifies for Supplemental Security Income (SSI) from the federal government, a Special Needs Trust can be established for them without impacting their SSI payments. For this kind of trust and others, it is wise to consult with an estate planning attorney with expertise in this area.

All trusts have something in common—they require at least one named trustee to manage their assets. Selecting a trustee is as important a decision as choosing an executor for your will (which we will look at next), perhaps more so. However, the selection criteria are very similar. Most large financial institutions have trust departments and would be more than happy to be named as the trustee due to the opportunity to earn management and transaction fees on the account.

If you choose a firm as the trustee, make sure you know exactly what services they will provide and at what cost.

Preparing a Will

A final thing we need to look at is the sensitive and sometimes emotional subject of preparing a will and your other essential documents. Regardless of your age, this is one of the most important aspects of legacy planning that you need to do. Finalizing your estate plan and getting specific documents like your will and other directives in place is an act of love and care for those you leave behind, especially since you'll be off rejoicing in heaven. Having these things in place will help to minimize the effort required to take care of your affairs at a difficult time when your loved ones are grieving over their loss. It's also a way to practice wise stewardship after you're gone by proactively taking steps to ensure—insofar as it depends on you—that the money and possessions God has given you are put to good use.

Wills Are Scriptural

Wills have been around for a long time; in fact, they are mentioned in the Bible: "Where a will exists, the death of the one who made it must be established. For a will is valid only when people die, since it is never in effect while the one who made it is living" (Heb. 9:16–17). The verse is out of context, but it does show that wills were commonplace in biblical times and functioned much as they do now. In another verse, the Bible reminds us to "put [our] affairs in order" (Isa. 38:1 HCSB), especially if we know the end is near. You can't communicate your wishes from heaven after you're gone, but with a will, you can lay out everything in writing in as much detail as you want (or need). If you don't, you may leave a chaotic situation behind for your family and the courts to sort out, and things may not go as you hoped.

Simplify Things

In addition to using a will, there are other things you can do to make things as simple and easy as possible by keeping your estate out of probate. This includes things like beneficiary designations on financial accounts and life insurance policies along with Transfer on Death (TOD) or Payable on Death (POD) provisions based on the situation. In doing this, you can put basic legal requirements in place with your financial institutions to ensure that your accounts go immediately to heirs without having to first go to probate. This is especially helpful for couples where the surviving spouse inherits all the assets, but it is wise to list contingent beneficiaries as well if they are not named in a will. In addition to beneficiary designations, using joint account ownership is a way to automatically transfer assets such as savings, houses, and vehicles.

Leaving IRA Assets

Most of us will have our retirement savings in a tax-deferred account, such as an IRA. Your heirs may also have an IRA. IRAs are like any other account when it comes to estate planning and your will. But they are also unique in the way your IRA assets can be passed on to heirs. This is where the Stretch IRA or Multigenerational IRA comes in.

> **Key Concept:** A *Stretch IRA* is an estate planning strategy that effectively extends the tax-deferred status of an inherited IRA when it is passed to a non-spouse beneficiary such as a son or daughter. It allows the inherited assets to continue to grow tax-free; however, the recipient will be required to take RMDs and pay taxes accordingly.

You may not be familiar with the term Stretch IRA, as it is not a type of IRA such as a Traditional, Roth, SEP, or SIMPLE. Instead, it is more of a financial and estate planning tool that can be used based on some recent changes in the tax code.

Some people will have to spend most of their savings in retirement, while others will have something left in their IRAs when they die. If children have been designated as beneficiaries, they won't have the option of transferring the assets into their own IRA, but they can move them into an inherited IRA, sometimes referred to as a beneficiary distribution account, and there are specific IRS rules that have to be followed. The most important is, in the case of a non-spouse inheritor, RMDs are usually required to start after the year of death and must be taken in full. Also, if the distributions are taxable, that must also be paid. But one of the key benefits is that distributions from an inherited non-spousal IRA taken before age 59½ are not subject to a 10-percent early withdrawal penalty. The inheritor's eventual course of action will be determined by their age, the age of the original owner, their income needs, any creditor protection concerns, and the type of IRA they inherit.

The stretch or multigenerational aspect of this provision is that the same kind of transfer can occur after the inheritor dies. Any remaining assets in the beneficiary distribution account can be passed to a named beneficiary, your grandson or granddaughter for example. In that sense, the lifetime of your original IRA can be stretched across multiple generations (if it survives that long).

Choosing Your Executor

Deciding who will make sure your wishes are honored and executed is one of the most important estate planning decisions you will make. You would typically name your personal representative or executor in your will, and he or she will be legally responsible for carrying out your wishes and administering your financial affairs after you are gone.

Ordinarily, when one spouse passes away, everything is left to the surviving spouse if the will is prepared accordingly. Additionally, if ownership of all financial accounts and significant assets has been set up as joint ownership/tenancy/title, including beneficiary designations, executorship is relatively straightforward, and everything should easily pass to the surviving spouse. If the surviving spouse isn't able to manage their affairs very well or is incapacitated after the will is written, a competent executor becomes more necessary. Should both spouses die at the same time, the role of the executor becomes mandatory.

Many people designate one of their children as executor. This is understandable and perfectly fine, but it is essential to ensure that they are up to the task. Regardless of who you choose, you and your spouse should agree and that the person can fully and faithfully execute your wishes. It may be wise to name a secondary executor to assist, especially if the executor is a younger family member. A good choice would be a CPA or family lawyer; just make sure they agree and will be available should you need them.

There are some basic criteria that you may want to consider when choosing an executor. First, they should have a general understanding of personal financial matters, including investments, inheritances, and financial transfers (or know how to get help on these areas). Second, they must be committed to implementing the desires and requirements of the will and dealing with any conflicting objectives any heirs may have. (This can be sensitive if the executor is one of your heirs; thus it may be wise for other family heirs to know that in advance.) Third, they need the diligence and discipline to file all of the required documents and reports—accurately, on-time, and per local statutes. If your chosen executor doesn't sufficiently meet all of these requirements, best to consider others.

A common dilemma is whether to choose a family member to act as executor. Not everyone is up to the task, and it may not be best to have an heir as an executor, depending on the family relationships and dynamics. The alternative is to designate a trusted friend or professional advisor. For unusually large or complicated estates, an attorney who specializes in estate law may be best. Something to consider, however, is that people move, change, grow older, and die, so you may want to revisit your decision from time to time (perhaps whenever you update your will). Be especially careful with using a small financial institution representative as they tend to merge or be acquired, resulting in employee displacements and other changes that you may not like. Another problem is a possible conflict of interest as financial firms have an inherent desire to increase their assets under management.

Other Essential Documents

In addition to a will, several other related documents need to be completed. The first is the *Health Care Directive*. This typically involves two documents: *Living Will* and *Health Care Power of Attorney*. Together, these documents help you to give direction regarding the medical decisions that are made at the end of life. This is important because most physicians are obligated to keep you alive regardless of the emotional and financial cost to your family, or your quality of life. These are highly personal decisions that are influenced by your experiences, values, and beliefs. By putting your wishes into writing, you can express your wishes to your family, who in turn can better navigate complicated and emotional end-of-life decisions.

Each of these documents serves a particular purpose. The *Living Will*[5] communicates your wishes under certain medical conditions, especially about end-of-life decisions related to heroic intervention, artificial life-support, and experimental treatments. The *Health Care Power of Attorney* authorizes someone to make medical decisions on your behalf and following the wishes in your Living Will in the event you are unable to do so (if you are in a coma, for example).

Another essential document is the *Durable Power of Attorney for Finances,* which you can use to name another person to act on your behalf concerning your financial matters if you are alive but incapacitated. Oftentimes, spouses grant each other such power, but it is also wise to name an alternate if both become incapacitated. This document can convey broad powers or can be limited to specific things such as collecting income and paying bills.

A final document that is just as important as the others is the *Information for Caregivers and Survivors.* I have one that I call the *"Letter from your husband who is now in heaven"* (yes, that's the actual title). This is the "open after I'm gone letter." In many ways, it is one of the loving and caring things you can do for your family. It contains all the financial and insurance account details and related information that my wife and/or an executor or personal representative needs to know if I am gone or incapacitated with a power of attorney in effect. This is not a legal document unless made a part of your will. The information frequently changes, so it makes sense to have it as a separate document. Most people don't ever write this letter because they don't want to think about the end of life (I admit, it is strange to write a letter while imagining that you are dead), or they just don't know where to start. But make no mistake about it—if you do, it will be *greatly* appreciated!

Summary

- *Living* a legacy is just as important as *leaving* a legacy. The former is how you impact others for their good and God's glory while you are living with the time, talents, and treasures you have been given; the latter deals mainly with guiding how your treasures (money and possessions) will be used for similar purposes after you are gone.

- Regardless of your age or season in life, a will is an excellent way to ensure that your wishes are followed after your passing. It provides clear direction to your survivors and heirs and should embody the same stewardship principles that you applied when making decisions when you were alive.

- In addition to a will, there are several other legal documents that need to be included to help address health care and financial concerns when we are no longer able to do so. Also, consider writing a letter to caregivers and survivors that provides them with all the detailed information they will need, in addition to what is in your will, to manage your affairs and carry out your wishes moving forward.

For Reflection

- Do you think of your legacy as more than just the money and possessions you leave behind when you die? What kind of a nonmaterial legacy do you want to leave?

- Have you procrastinated putting together a will and the other final documents discussed in this chapter? If so, why? What steps can you take right away to get started?

CONCLUSION

I want to end this book with an appeal: Work hard, save diligently, invest wisely; but please don't retire, at least not in the most traditional sense of the word. Instead, reimagine retirement as something different from what the world envisions.

You can leave your full-time job or a lifelong career and retire, but if you do, make sure you are ready for it. Make sure you can fund your retirement and have a plan to make your money last. Take care of things like health care and long-term care if you need to. But no matter what, please don't retire from the church, your family, or your community. Don't retire from God's army. Stay on mission: keep serving, keep giving, keep sharing your life and resources with others. This is the disciples' way of life in the last season of life.

> **Don't retire, at least not in the most traditional sense of the word. Instead, reimagine retirement as something different from what the world envisions.**

For the Christian, retirement is an opportunity to do more of what we have already been doing in service to God and others, all the way to the end. As the apostle Paul encourages us in 1 Corinthians 15:58: "Therefore, my dear brothers and sisters, be steadfast, immovable, always excelling in the Lord's work, because you know that your labor in the Lord is not in vain."

There are many paths a person can follow in retirement. For those of us who have been changed by the gospel, our calling and purpose are already clear: to invest ourselves in the lives of others, both within and without the church, and to persevere in godly zeal as we grow old so that we can finish well to the glory of God (2 Tim. 4:7). Retirement is not a time to neglect the mission we have been called to and get to be a part of. Our primary goals should not be learning how to paint or improving our golf score (although there's certainly nothing wrong with painting or playing golf—my wife is great at the former and I stink at the latter); it should have more to do with finishing well so we can hear the words, "Well done, good and faithful servant!" (Matt. 25:23a).

One of the great blessings we receive as believers is that God, our heavenly Father, will be with us throughout our lives, and that he has a plan and a purpose for each and every day: "'For I know the plans I have for you'—this is the LORD's declaration—'plans for your well-being, not for disaster, to give you a future and a hope'" (Jer. 29:11). Let us rejoice in the great hope we have been given and "live [our lives in a manner] worthy of the gospel of Christ" (Phil. 1:27a).

APPENDIX: RESOURCES

Stewardship and Generosity Ministries

- Compass—Finances God's Way: www.Compass1.org
- Crown Financial Ministries: www.Crown.org
- Generous Giving: www.GenerousGiving.org
- Eternal Purpose Ministries (Randy Alcorn): https://www.epm.org/
- Freed Up in Later Life: https://goodsensemovement.org/resources/freed-up-in-later-life/
- Sound Mind Investing: https://soundmindinvesting.com/
- Ramsey Solutions: www.DaveRamsey.com
- Retirement Stewardship: www.retirementstewardship.com
- Ron Blue's Resources: www.Lifeway.com/GodOwnsItAll
- Sound Mind Investing: www.SoundMindInvesting.com

Financial Services Providers

- Annuities (SPIAs): https://www.immediateannuities.com/
- Betterment: https://www.betterment.com/
- Fidelity Investments: https://fidelity.com/

- Schwab: https://www.schwab.com/
- TIAA: https://www.tiaa.org/public
- USAA: https://www.usaa.com/
- Vanguard: https://investor.vanguard.com/home/
- Wealthfront: https://www.wealthfront.com/

Financial Calculators

- CalcXML: https://www.calcxml.com/english.htm
- Dinkytown.net: https://www.dinkytown.net/
- Esplanner: https://basic.esplanner.com/
- Investopedia: https://www.investopedia.com/calculator/
- New Retirement: https://newretirement.com
- SmartAsset: https://smartasset.com/retirement/

Budgeting and Money Management Tools

- Banktivity (Mac software): https://www.iggsoftware.com/
- Every Dollar: https://www.everydollar.com/
- Neo budget: https://neobudget.com/
- Mint.com: https://www.mint.com/
- Mvelopes: https://www.mvelopes.com/
- Quicken: https://www.quicken.com/
- Wally: http://wally.me/
- YNAB: https://www.youneedabudget.com/

Financial Dashboards

- On Trajectory: https://www.ontrajectory.com/welcome.html

- Personal Capital: https://www.personalcapital.com/

Social Security and Medicare Resources

- Maximize my Social Security: https://maximizemyso cialsecurity.com/
- Medicare: https://www.medicare.gov/
- Open Social Security (Calculator): https://opensocialsecu rity.com/
- Social Security Administration: https://www.ssa.gov/

Work Resources

- 48 Days: https://www.48days.com/
- Encore Careers: https://encore.org/
- Crossroads: https://www.crossroadscareer.org

NOTES

Introduction

1. "Employee Financial Wellness Survey 2018 results," PwC, accessed October 22, 2018, https://www.pwc.com/us/en/private-company-services/publications/assets/pwc-2018-employee-wellness-survey.pdf.

Chapter 1

1. This is particularly true for elderly parents or other relatives who are unable to provide for themselves through no fault of their own.

2. "Economic Security for Seniors Facts," National Council on Aging, accessed June 8, 2018, https://www.ncoa.org/news/resources-for-reporters/get-the-facts/economic-security-facts/.

3. Patrick W. Seburn, "Evolution of Employee-Provided Defined Benefit Plans," US Department of Labor, Bureau of Labor Statistics, accessed June 12, 2018, https://www.bls.gov/mlr/1991/12/art3full.pdf.

4. "How a Different America Responded to the Great Depression," Pew Research Center, accessed June 15, 2018, http://www.pewresearch.org/2010/12/14/how-a-different-america-responded-to-the-great-depression/.

5. "Social Security History: Life Expectancy for Social Security," Social Security Administration, https://www.ssa.gov/history/lifeexpect.html.

6. "Actuarial Life Table—Period Life Table, 2016," Social Security Administration, https://www.ssa.gov/oact/STATS/table4c6.html.

7. "About Form 4361," US Government, Internal Revenue Service, accessed June 21, 2018, https://www.irs.gov/uac/about-form-4361.

8. The Social Security Administration (SSA) defines *full retirement age* as "the age at which a person may first become entitled to full or unreduced retirement benefits."

9. Irena Dushi, Howard M. Iams, and Brad Trenkamp, "The Importance of Social Security Benefits to the Income of the Aged Population," Social Security Administration, accessed June 22, 2018, https://www.ssa.gov/policy/docs/ssb/v77n2/v77n2p1.html.

10. Willis Towers Watson and Brendan McFarland, "A Continuing Shift in Retirement Offerings in the Fortune 500," accessed on June 22, 2018, https://www.towerswatson.com/en-US/Insights/Newsletters/Americas/insider/2016/02/a-continuing-shift-in-retirement-offerings-in-the-fortune-500.

11. "Snapshot: Average American Predicts Retirement Age of 66," Gallup, accessed July 12, 2018, https://news.gallup.com/poll/234302/snapshot-americans-project-average-retirement-age.aspx.

12. For the year 1900 versus 2000, there was a 60 percent increase for white men and 106 percent increase for black men, and a 63 percent increase for white women and 121 percent increase for black women. Data Sources: National Vital Statistics Reports, Vol. 50, No. 6. Life Expectancy at Birth, by Race and Sex, Selected Years 1929–98; National Vital Statistics Reports, Vol. 49, No. 12. Deaths, Preliminary Data for 2000; US Census Bureau. P23–190 Current Population Reports: Special Studies. 65+ in the United States.

13. According to the Social Security Administration, increasing life expectancies means that someone who retires at age 45 today may need to fund 45 years in retirement as there is about a 20 percent chance they could live to age 90 or longer.

14. Maryalene LaPonsie, "How to Reset a Retirement Gone Wrong," *U.S. News and World Report*, accessed July 5, 2018, https://money.usnews.com/money/retirement/baby-boomers/articles/2017-11-30/how-to-reset-a-retirement-gone-wrong.

15. "Work in Retirement: 2014," New Age/Merrill Lynch, accessed July 5, 2018, https://www.ml.com/publish/content/application/pdf/GWMOL/MLWM_Work-in-Retirement_2014.pdf.

16. Blake Ellis, "Average American Inheritance: $177,000," CNN Money, accessed June 30, 2018, http://money.cnn.com/2013/12/13/retirement/american-inheritance/index.html.

17. "The 2017 Retirement Confidence Survey: Many Workers Lack Retirement Confidence and Feel Stressed about Retirement Preparations," Employee Benefit Research Institute, accessed on June 30, 2018, https://www.ebri.org/content/the-2017-retirement-confidence-survey-many-workers-lack-retirement-confidence-and-feel-stressed-about-retirement-preparations-3426.

18. "Retirement Security: Most Households Approaching Retirement Have Low Savings," US Government Accountability Office, accessed July 2, 2018, http://www.gao.gov/products/GAO-15-419.

19. Alicia H. Mennell and Geoffrey Sanzenbacher, "National Retirement Risk Index Shows Modest Improvement in 2016," Center for Retirement Research at Boston College, accessed July 2, 2018, http://crr.bc.edu/briefs/national-retirement-risk-index-shows-modest-improvement-in-2016/.

Chapter 2

1. "Longevity in the Ancient World," Early Church History, accessed July 6, 2018, https://earlychurchhistory.org/daily-life/longevity-in-the-ancient-world/.

2. This idea of "biblical principles" rests in the fact that the Bible, as the final authority for all things, is the means by which God provides both explicit and implicit guidance for living in a way that keeps us from wrong thinking and behavior and toward the active pursuit of a lifestyle that honors and glorifies him. Although different from application, biblical interpretation helps us to identify timeless biblical principles that can be applied in a modern context and to our everyday lives and to present-day situations about which the Bible is otherwise relatively silent.

3. Webster's dictionary defines it as "withdrawal from one's position or occupation or from active working life."

4. Timothy Keller, *Every Good Endeavor* (New York: Dutton, a Member of Penguin Group (USA) Inc., 2012), 34–35.

5. Walter A. Elwell, ed., *The Evangelical Dictionary of Theology, 2nd Edition* (Grand Rapids, MI: Baker Academic, 2009), 1149.

6. Ibid., 1279–80.

7. This is taken from the working definition I use for "retirement stewardship" on my blog: https://www.retirementstewardship.com/2016/05/20/what-is-retirement-stewardship/.

Chapter 3

1. First Corinthians is an excellent study on our Christian "liberty" to do or not do certain things, but not in a way the ignores biblical values and priorities and what it means to live life as a disciple of Jesus Christ.

2. Larry Burkett and Ron Blue, *Your Money After the Big 5-0* (Nashville, TN: B&H Publishing, 2007), 67.

3. Timothy Keller, *Shaped by the Gospel* (Grand Rapids, MI: Zondervan, 2016), 65.

4. Matthew Henry, *Matthew Henry's Commentary: Acts to Revelation, Volume VI* (McClean, VA: Macdonald Publishing Company, 1988), 861.

5. Here I use the word *calling* in the context of 1 Corinthians 7:17: "Let each one live his life in the situation the Lord assigned when God called him. This is what I command in all the churches." It refers to the general "callings" that we all have as well as the specific "calling" to do something based on what God has uniquely equipped and gifted someone to do.

6. Jaime Munson, *Money: God or Gift* (www.theMoneyMission.com, 2014), Kindle edition, 35.

7. Ibid., 19.

8. Anonymous quote.

9. Billy Graham, "Don't Retire from Life," Faith Gateway, accessed July 14, 2018, http://www.faithgateway.com/dont-retire-from-life/#.WqfdAiXwapp.

Chapter 4

1. Ron Blue with Michael Blue, *Master Your Money* (Chicago, IL: Moody Publishers, 2016), 39.

2. These recommendations have been consistently taught by other Christian stewardship teachers such as Larry Burkett, Howard Dayton, Chuck Bentley, and Dave Ramsey.

3. Ron Blue rightly includes giving as one of five short-term uses for our income, which also includes living expenses, debt repayment, taxes, and short- or long-term saving (which he describes as "cash-flow margin").

4. Some teachers, like Dave Ramsey, recommend an even lower percentage of 25 percent. This is ideal if you can manage it as it contributes to greater margin in your financial situation. He is also a big proponent of the fifteen-year mortgage.

5. Claire Tsosie and Erin El Issa, "2017 American Household Credit Card Debt Study," (based on an online survey conducted Nov. 8–10, 2017 in the US by Harris Poll), accessed August 4, 2018, https://www.nerdwallet.com/blog/average-credit-card-debt-household/.

6. Dave Ramsey, "What Is a Budget?" accessed August 5, 2018, https://www.daveramsey.com/blog/what-is-a-budget.

7. There are a few products that I recommend that can help you create a budget and stick to it. Check out the resources section in the appendix for more information.

Chapter 5

1. This is why having low-cost term life insurance is such an excellent way to love and provide for your family in case the unthinkable should happen.

2. "Monthly Statistical Snapshot, September 2018," Social Security Administration, accessed September 6, 2018, https://www.ssa.gov/policy/docs/quickfacts/stat_snapshot/.

3. The math of the compounding effect is such that even those who invest large sums much later in life don't do as well either.

4. William G. Gale, Hilary Gelfond, and Jason Fichtner, "How Will Retirement Saving Change by 2050? Prospects for the Millennial Generation," Economic Studies at Brooking, https://www.brookings.edu/wp-content/uploads/2019/03/How-Will-Retirement-Saving-Change-by-2050.docx.pdf, 8.

5. The report also points out multiple factors that may be contributing to this, including the slow recovery from the 2008 recession and high student loan debt.

6. Jennifer Erin Brown, M.S., J.D., LL.M., "Millennials and Retirement: Already Falling Short," National Institute of Retirement Security, https://www.nirsonline.org/wp-content/uploads/2018/02/Millennials-Report-1.pdf, 1.

7. It is important to note that the annual contribution limits can change from year to year. The most authoritative information is available from the IRS at https://www.irs.gov/retirement-plans/plan-participant-employee/retirement-topics-contributions.

8. Bengen's work was originally published in his book, *Conserving Client Portfolios During Retirement* (Denver, CO: FPA Press, 2006).

9. For more information, see *The 4 Percent Rule Is Not Safe in a Low-Yield World*, by Michael Finke, Ph.D., Wade D. Pfau, Ph.D., and David M. Blanchett, CFP, CFA, https://www.onefpa.org/journal/Pages/The%204%20Percent%20Rule%20Is%20Not%20Safe%20in%20a%20Low-Yield%20World.aspx.

10. The simple equation for this table is (Desired Spending Level – Social Security and/or Pension) x 25 = Amount Needed to Retire. (The 25x multiplier is based on a 4 percent withdrawal rate. For a withdrawal rate of 5 percent, the multiplier would be 20x; a 3 percent rate would equate to a multiplier of 30x.)

11. You can access the tool directly here: https://www.fidelity.com/products/retirement/widget/xfactor/retire_xfactor.html

12. "Retirement Topics—Catch-Up Contributions," Internal Revenue Service, accessed September 17, 2018, https://www.irs.gov/retirement-plans/plan-participant-employee/retirement-topics-catch-up-contributions.

Chapter 6

1. Wayne Grudem, *Christian Ethics* (Wheaton, IL: Crossway, 2018), 1033.

2. Larry Burkett and Ron Blue, *Your Money After the Big 5-0* (Nashville, TN: B&H Publishing, 2007), 115–16.

3. Dr. Grudem explains the difference by comparing the purchase of a stock with buying a lottery ticket. With the former, there is some probability of loss, but the likelihood of losing the lottery is often greater than 99 percent and the "probability of losing your entire investment in a widely diversified group of stocks is far less than 1 percent" (*Christian Ethics*, 1035–36).

4. Fidelity Investments just introduced four zero-expense ratio index funds (https://www.fidelity.com/mutual-funds/investing-ideas/index-funds).

5. "Morningstar Target Risk Allocation," Morningstar, accessed September 28, 2018, https://corporate.morningstar.com/US/documents/Indexes/TargetRiskIndexAllocationSummary.pdf.

Chapter 7

1. Some retirement calculators are listed in the appendix section.

2. "Retirement Estimator," US Government, Social Security Administration, accessed on September 24, 2018, https://www.ssa.gov/benefits/retirement/estimator.html.

3. The Federal Deposit Insurance Corporation (FDIC) is the United States government corporation that insures certain kinds of bank deposits.

4. Theoretically, these accounts could even go to zero in the most extreme (think "catastrophic") economic circumstances. Although large market losses of as much as 50 percent or more have happened, they are historically very rare. For all securities, and therefore companies and world currency, to become virtually worthless would require a cataclysmic economic meltdown. Only an "end-of-the-age" type of event could trigger such an occurrence.

Chapter 8

1. "Plan for a Long Retirement," The Vanguard Group, Inc., accessed on October 2, 2018, https://personal.vanguard.com/us/insights/retirement/plan-for-a-long-retirement-tool?lang=en.

2. This strategy, which is becoming increasingly popular, was originally derived from an article titled "The Theory of Life-Cycle Saving and Investing," originally published by the Federal Reserve Bank of Boston. It can be downloaded here: https://www.bostonfed.org/publications/public-policy-discussion-paper/2007/the-theory-of-life-cycle-saving-and-investing.aspx.

3. We looked at *Deferred Income Annuities* in chapter 5. These are usually purchased in the years preceding retirement and can be either the fixed income or variable and fixed-index variety.

4. At this writing, the "real yield" of a newly issued 5-year TIPS bond was 1.129 percent, which is the highest in about ten years. Source: https://tipswatch.com/2018/12/20/5-year-tips-reopening-gets-real-yield-of-1-129-highest-in-nearly-10-years/.

5. I own the iShares Barclays TIPS Bond ETF (TIP), for example, but these funds are also available from Fidelity, Vanguard, Schwab, and other asset managers.

6. Studies have shown that "real spending declines by an average of about 1 percent/year in the first decade of retirement, 2 percent/year in the second decade, and about 1 percent/year again in the final decade.

Given that inflation itself averages more than 2 percent per year through most of the historical years in the data set, though, this still means that retirees were maintaining or slightly increasing their *nominal* spending each year. Just by less than the annual amount of inflation." Michael Kitces, "Using Age Banding to Estimate How Spending Will Decline in Retirement," accessed November 15, 2018, https://www.kitces.com/blog/age-banding-by-basu-to-model-retirement-spending-needs-by-category/.

7. For more detailed information on early withdrawal rules, refer to IRS Publication #575, *Pension and Annuity Income*, https://www.irs.gov/forms-pubs/about-publication-575.

8. We discussed rebalancing in chapter 6 (investing). There is no set schedule for rebalancing a portfolio, but most professionals recommend that you at least consider it once a year. Rebalancing provides an added benefit: it gives you the opportunity to sell high and buy low, assuming you are willing to do that as many investors have a hard time selling assets that are doing well.

9. It should be noted once again that many financial professionals now say that the 4 percent rule needs to be adjusted to the 3 percent rule due to increased longevity and lower anticipated market returns over the next few decades.

10. You can look up CAPE here: http://www.multpl.com/shiller-pe/.

11. For more information, refer to IRS Publication 590-B, Distributions from Individual Retirement Accounts (IRAs), https://www.irs.gov/publications/p590b#en_US_2017_publink1000231258.

12. This strategy is part of what Steve Vernon, an actuary and research scholar at the Stanford Center on Longevity, termed the Spend Safely in Retirement Strategy (SS/RMD), which proposes delaying Social Security benefits until age 70, withdrawing no more than 3.5 percent starting at age 65 or 66, and then draws down using the IRS RMD percentages beginning at age 70. You can learn more about this strategy here: http://longevity.stanford.edu/wp-content/uploads/2017/12/How-to-pensionize-any-IRA-401k-final.pdf.

13. Money withdrawn from a taxable IRA cannot then be deposited into a nontaxable Roth IRA. The IRS requires that you have "earned income" to be eligible to contribute to a Roth account.

Chapter 9

1. According to a 2015 publication by the Social Security Administration titled "Expenditures of the Aged Chartbook, 2015," housing was the largest component of expenditures (35%) for households aged 65 or older; https://www.ssa.gov/policy/docs/chartbooks/expenditures_aged/2015/index.html.

2. My wife often creates something and gives it to a friend or family member as an expression of love and appreciation. I love seeing the looks on their faces when they receive the gift. For some reason, a creative gift from her hands tends to have a greater impact on the recipient than something she might have picked up in a store.

3. Rieva Lesonsky, "Forget Retirement—Many Baby Boomers Are Starting Small Businesses Instead," *Forbes*, https://www.forbes.com/sites/allbusiness/2018/07/19/baby-boomers-starting-small-businesses/.

4. https://www.kauffman.org/~/media/kauffman_org/microsites/kauffman_index/startup_activity_2016/kauffman_index_startup_activity_national_trends_2016.pdf.

5. A Title 1 school is a school receiving federal funds due to having a large concentration of low-income students. Those supplemental funds assist the school in meeting students' educational goals. In our city, these schools actively seek volunteer involvement from the church community, and there are several people from my church who serve there in different ways every week.

6. You can find more information about each of these "parts" at https://www.medicare.gov/sign-up-change-plans/decide-how-to-get-medicare/whats-medicare/what-is-medicare.html.

7. https://www.fidelity.com/about-fidelity/employer-services/a-couple-retiring-in-2018-would-need-estimated-280000.

8. You can read more about this approach here: https://www.specialneedsalliance.org/the-voice/funding-a-special-needs-trust-with-life-insurance-2/.

9. According to the US government, "Someone turning age 65 today has almost a 70 percent chance of needing some type of long-term care services and supports in their remaining years. Women need care longer (3.7 years) than men (2.2 years). One-third of today's 65-year-olds may never need long-term care support, but 20 percent will need it for longer

than 5 years." Source: https://longtermcare.acl.gov/the-basics/how-much-care-will-you-need.html.

10. IRS New Release, "IRS Provides Tax Inflation Adjustments for Tax Year 2019," https://www.irs.gov/newsroom/irs-provides-tax-inflation-adjustments-for-tax-year-2019.

11. In this example, 85 percent of the $25,000 Social Security benefit is taxable, which makes adjusted gross income $46,250. That, minus the standard deduction of $24,400, leaves taxable income of $21,850, which is taxed at 10 percent up to $19,400 ($1,940) and 12 percent of the remainder ($294), for a total tax of $2,234, or 4.8 percent of AGI of $46,250.

12. You can learn more about IRS withholding rules at https://www.irs.gov/taxtopics/tc306.

13. IRS publication 590 describes the rules on distributions from IRAs. Since the IRS and Congress change the rules almost yearly, it is a good idea to check this out before you make any decisions on distributions or rollovers.

Chapter 10

1. Larry Burkett and Ron Blue, *Your Money After the Big 5-0* (Nashville, TN: B&H Publishing, 2007),200.

2. Dave Ramsey, *The Legacy Journey* (Brentwood, TN: Ramsey Press, 2014), 138.

3. Ibid.

4. Burkett and Blue, *Your Money After the Big 5-0,* 205.

5. A Living Will may also be known as Advanced Health Care Directive, Personal Directive, Advance Directive, Medical Directive, or Advance Directive. In the United States, it has legal status in itself, but in other countries, it is used as a persuasive document in a legal context.